STEAMBOATS
ON
KEUKA LAKE

STEAMBOATS

⸭⸙⮞ ON ⮜⸘⸰

KEUKA LAKE

Penn Yan, Hammondsport and the Heart of the Finger Lakes

RICHARD S. MACALPINE
& CHARLES R. MITCHELL

THE
History
PRESS

Published by The History Press
Charleston, SC 29403
www.historypress.net

All images are from the collection of the Yates County History Center.

First published 2015

ISBN 978.1.54021.249.8

Library of Congress Control Number: 2015935123

Notice: The information in this book is true and complete to the best of our knowledge. It is
offered without guarantee on the part of the authors or The History Press. The authors and
The History Press disclaim all liability in connection with the use of this book.

This book is dedicated to the Yates County History Center (aka the Yates County Genealogical and Historical Society), the fourth-oldest county historical society in the state of New York, founded in 1860. The History Center maintains three museums at the corner of Main and Chapel Streets in Penn Yan: the Oliver House Museum, the L. Caroline Underwood Museum and the Scherer Carriage House. Its mission over all those years has been to collect, preserve and promote the rich and varied history of Yates County. All royalties from the sale of this book go to help it accomplish that mission.

CONTENTS

Acknowledgements   9
Introduction. Recapture the Romance of the
    Steamboat Era on Keuka Lake   11

1. The Early Years on Crooked Lake   15
2. The Golden Age of Steam (1865–1915)   21
3. The Steamboat Wars (1872–1892)   25
4. The Keuka Steamers   37
5. A Virtual Excursion on the Lake, Circa 1900   79
6. Actual Excursions   119
7. Grapes and Wine   129
8. The End of an Era   137

Notes   145
Bibliography   149
Index   153
About the Authors   157

ACKNOWLEDGEMENTS

O ur major resource for this project was the excellent collection of the Yates County History Center in Penn Yan, New York. It is the fourth-oldest county historical society in the state of New York, having been originally established in 1860. It was dormant for several years in the late nineteenth and early twentieth centuries but was revived in 1928 and has been growing and going strong ever since. Over the years, the collection went from being kept in the homes of the officers to being stored in the basement of the Penn Yan Public Library in the early 1930s. In the summer of 1948, the Village of Penn Yan, which owned the Oliver House on Main Street, allowed the historical society to move its collection into the five rooms on the second floor of the building. Eventually, it took over the entire building. In 2002, the historical society acquired the use of the house next door on Chapel Street that became the L. Caroline Underwood Museum. In 2011, it renovated the old garage behind the Underwood Museum and turned it into the Scherer Carriage House. Each time, the expansion was necessitated by the increase in the size of the collection. We made ample use of its subject files, which included the different boats, landings, resorts, etc. The finest of its photo collection, which pertained to the steamboat era, will be found throughout this book. Finally, its collection of old newspapers such as the *Yates County Chronicle* and the *Penn Yan Democrat* allowed us to get the feel for the time period, as well as gain specific information about the boats.

Very few historians operate in a vacuum; most build on the work of others. Such was the case with us. One of the problems with researching the steamboat era was the amazing number of discrepancies when it comes to specifics: dates when events occurred, where incidents took place, the length of the boats, etc. In order to maintain accuracy, we had to constantly cross-reference. One of our go-to sources for this, other than the old issues of local newspapers, was the substantial research done over the years by Don Quant of Port Byron, New York. We especially made use of Don's research on two steamers, the *Cricket* and the *Lulu*. The other resource was Steven Harvey, who now lives in North Carolina. In 2010, he wrote *It Started with a Steamboat: An American Saga*, which covered the steamboat era on all the Finger Lakes. In doing his research, he went through old editions of the *Hammondsport Herald* between 1878 and 1918, and we used his notes as a resource.

We would also like to thank Bob Canfield, former historian for the town of Wayne and member of the Wayne History Group. Bob shared photos and information with us relating to the Keuka Hotel and Bessie Young.

Finally, we would like to thank our wives, Jeanie MacAlpine and Melissa Mitchell, for their support, careful proofreading and constructive criticism.

Introduction

RECAPTURE THE ROMANCE OF THE STEAMBOAT ERA ON KEUKA LAKE

Family history got me interested in the steamboat era on Keuka Lake. One of my great-great-grandfathers was Nelson Retan, who owned a basket factory in Pulteney, New York, just up the hill from the lake. He was also a Civil War veteran and was an active member of the Union army veterans' group, the Grand Army of the Republic (GAR). I ran across a story in an 1890 local newspaper in which the members of his GAR post and their wives went down to Pulteney Landing on the west branch of Keuka Lake and boarded the steamer *Urbana*. They went around the end of Bluff Point into the east branch to a resort hotel named O-go-ya-go. They had a fine dinner there and then reboarded the *Urbana* and went on a moonlight cruise. Also on board the boat was "the Italian band" with its violins and harps. The veterans and their wives cruised and danced into the early morning hours. My thought was, "Wow! Wouldn't it be great to do something like that? How romantic!" That story got me interested in the steamboats on Keuka.

For many years, the Yates County History Center in Penn Yan, New York, sponsored a Steamboat Era Cruise on Keuka Lake. That's how I connected with Charles R. Mitchell on this topic. Chuck had been a professional photographer and owned a shop on Main Street in Penn Yan called the Photographic Center. Seeing what digital photography was going to do to his business, he sold it and became the curator at the Yates County History Center. Combining his knowledge of photography and his love of history, Chuck focused on organizing and preserving the ten thousand or so images in the history center's collection. Along the way, he authored three books on Keuka Lake in Arcadia Publishing's Images of America Series. The research that he did on the photos for those books made him very familiar with the steamboat era on Keuka. I teamed up with Chuck and shared narration duties for the Steamboat Era Cruise starting in 2008. We held the cruises on one of the tour boats on the lake, and each cruise served as both an educational program and a fundraiser for us. Our slogan was "Recapture the Romance of the Steamboat Era on Keuka Lake." Each year, we did more research in old issues of local newspapers on the boats, the landings, the resorts and events of the time for our three-hour narration. Each year, the event sold out and there was usually a waiting list in case of last-minute cancellations.

The situation with tour boats on Keuka Lake has changed dramatically. Where once there were three, as of this writing there are none. In the summer of 2005, there was a terrible accident on Lake George in eastern New York. A tour boat, the *Ethan Allen*, tipped over with a near-capacity crowd on board. Most of the passengers were senior citizens, many in wheelchairs. The result was twenty deaths and a number of lawsuits. New York State passed a new series of tough regulations and inspections for tour boats operating on the state's waters. The first tour boat to leave Keuka Lake was the *Viking Spirit*, which the History Center had used for several years. It was owned by the Viking Resort on the east branch of the lake. New regulations established that hulls with marine plywood have to be replaced if they are more than twenty years old. Rather than face the expense of replacing the hull on their aging boat, the owners decided to scrap it. Next to leave was the *Keuka Maid*, another aging boat that was based at the southern end of the lake. We never used the *Keuka Maid*, but it was always an option. Again, the owner was required to hire a huge crane to lift the boat out of the water to inspect the hull. Rather than face the expense, he decided to have it scrapped. That left one tour boat on the lake, the *Esperanza Rose*, based in Branchport on the west branch and owned by David and Lisa Wegman, who also owned the Esperanza Mansion. We used the *Rose* for several years and had some very successful cruises on it. We had a wonderful relationship with the people who owned and managed it. However, late in 2013, it was announced that the boat had "inspection issues" that would require $35,000 to correct. David Wegman decided to retire the boat from service as a result. It was scrapped in the fall of 2014.

That left the Yates County History Center with a great idea and no way to carry it out. Early in 2014, I approached Chuck Mitchell with the idea of taking all that we had accumulated over the years in terms of information, stories and photographs and turning it into a book. He agreed enthusiastically. As curator, Chuck knows what the History Center has available for relevant photographs of the era. His past experiences as a professional photographer and proprietor of the Photographic Center on Main Street in Penn Yan gave him the expertise to bring aged and faded images from the nineteenth century back to life. The research I did during the five years that I was the main narrator on our cruises meant that I had a storehouse of information and stories from the era. Chuck and I have worked to combine the photos and the information in a way that will allow readers to "Recapture the Romance of the Steamboat Era."

RICH MACALPINE
Penn Yan, New York

Chapter I

THE EARLY YEARS ON CROOKED LAKE

There are eleven lakes in the Finger Lakes region of New York State, from Conesus Lake south of Rochester to Otisco Lake not far from Syracuse. Located smack-dab in the middle of the region is Keuka Lake—five lakes to the east of it and five lakes to the west. One can rattle off the basic facts describing the lake: the only Y-shaped lake, twenty miles long, an average width of three-quarters of a mile, about sixty miles of shoreline, 186 feet at its deepest point, located at 715 feet above sea level, etc. But quantifying the lake doesn't really describe it. People who live or vacation here would say there is a certain aesthetic quality or spirit to the lake that is hard to describe. Many have tried over the years in the form of poetry, flowery descriptions, paintings or photographs. There is a strong tendency to romanticize Keuka and believe that it is unique, as in this excerpt from the *Yates County Chronicle* in August 1897: "The class of people who patronize Lake Keuka, with the fullest realization of its charms, are the lovers of the beautiful in nature, who appreciate all that the Creator has bestowed upon it and know how to get pleasure out of every daylight moment, and invigorating and restful sleep out of the calm, cool evenings." Presently, there are over eleven thousand people on the I ♥ Keuka Lake Facebook page who post photos of sunrises, sunsets, good times on the lake and beautiful scenery. People on that page wax nostalgic about their childhood experiences on the lake, businesses that have come and gone or one-hundred-year-old cottages that have been torn down and replaced by modern buildings. Among these modern-day denizens of Keuka Lake, there is an unusual interest in the history and lore of the lake.

This Keuka Lake aerial is looking south with Penn Yan in the foreground, Hammondsport to the south and Branchport to the right, around the bluff.

Keuka was the name given to the lake by the Senecas of the Iroquois Nation. It means "canoe landing." There were early native settlements on the northern ends of both the east and west branches. When white settlers started coming into the area in the late 1700s, they called it "Crooked Lake," and it kept that name until a few years after the Civil War, when it was decided to return to the native name. It was "Lake Keuka" in the late nineteenth and early twentieth centuries and "Keuka Lake" in more recent years.

Other than the canoes of the Senecas, the first boats on the lake were ferries that moved people and goods between the east and west sides of the lake, as well as to Bluff Point. One of the first of these was operated by Hiram Gleason. On what today is Marlena Point, then known as Gleason's Point, on the east side across from Bluff Point, he built a home in 1821 and had a farm and a tavern. Hiram had the only ferry service on the lake for a while. It ran from the east side of the lake to the west side with a stop on the end of Bluff Point. Gleason's ferry was powered in part by two horses on treadmills with paddle wheels on each side of the boat. It was large enough to carry four teams of horses and their wagons. It must have been a sight to see. He operated it until his death in 1835, which was the same year the first steamboat appeared on the lake.

Starting in the late 1820s, there was talk in the village of Penn Yan and in Albany about building a canal to connect Penn Yan on Keuka Lake to Dresden on Seneca Lake. That touched off a local version of "canal fever" as Penn Yan businessmen envisioned their village becoming a commercial center and area farmers looked for expanded markets. Keuka Lake could connect to the Erie Canal through Seneca Lake and eventually to the world. The charter was issued, and construction on the Crooked Lake Canal began in the spring of 1831. A combination of labor problems and engineering challenges meant that it took longer than expected to complete. The engineering challenge was that the canal had to rise nearly 280 feet in elevation on its eight-mile route from Dresden to the entrance of Keuka Lake. That required a total of twenty-eight locks to be built, which greatly increased the cost of construction. Late in 1833, the canal began operations.

When plans for construction of the canal became definite in 1829, enterprising businessmen saw an opportunity on Keuka Lake. Canalboats coming up from Dresden would have to be towed on the lake in order to service area farmers. The Crooked Lake Steamboat Company was formed, and construction began on the first steamboat for the lake. Named the *Keuka*, it was ready for service in 1835. It consisted of two Durham boats connected by a center cabin and a center paddle wheel. A Durham boat was used in the famous painting of George Washington crossing the Delaware River on Christmas Eve 1776. The *Keuka* looked similar to a large pontoon boat or a catamaran. It was eighty feet long and was used mainly for towing canalboats and rafts of logs on the lake. In 1848, one of its pilots, allegedly intoxicated, ran the boat aground near Hammondsport, and it had to be dismantled.

While the *Keuka* was still in operation, it was decided by Hammondsport businessmen to build a new boat that would rival in size and quality the boats that were beginning to appear on other Finger Lakes. They hired a boat builder from New York City to manage the construction. In late June 1845, the steamer *Steuben* was launched at Hammondsport. The *Steuben* was 132 feet long, 35 feet at its greatest width and had a fifty-horsepower steam engine. It was put into service that August. Its first captain was thirty-four-year-old John Gregg. Born in Ireland, Gregg started his steamboat career as the engineer on the *Keuka* and toward the end of that boat's service was its captain. He would captain the *Steuben* for nearly twenty years, acquiring ownership of the boat along the way. Gregg was described as an affable, urbane man who had many friends and loyal customers. After the dismantling of the *Keuka*, the *Steuben* was the only steamer on the lake for those twenty years. Captain Gregg continued hauling freight and towing canalboats, but he made a major effort to build up the passenger trade during the summers.

During the Civil War, the *Steuben* ran a regular schedule between Penn Yan and Hammondsport and ran special excursions for school groups, church groups and other organizations during summers. Before the busy season in the spring of 1864, Gregg decided to sell his boat "and all its prerogatives" (mainly docking rights). It was starting to show its age, and Gregg was developing other interests. Grape agriculture and the wine industry were undergoing rapid expansion on the shores of the lake. In 1862, he became an agent for the Pleasant Valley Wine Company. Newspapers of the time reported that Captain Gregg was going into the grape-growing business on Bluff Point.

The buyer of the *Steuben* was Allen Wood, who had gotten into the steamboat business on Canandaigua Lake. Starting in 1854, he and his brother owned and operated the side-wheeler steamer *Joseph Wood*. He sold his interests in that in 1862 and moved to Hammondsport. At the time he bought the *Steuben*, the *Ontario Times* reported: "We congratulate the good people of Penn Yan upon the prospective improvement of the steamboat interest upon their beautiful lake. Captain Wood understands his business perfectly and will leave nothing undone that will tend to promote the convenience and comfort of those he has to depend upon for patronage and support. It will not be his fault if Crooked Lake is not soon made a more attractive place of resort than ever before." After buying the *Steuben*, Captain Wood lined up Benjamin and Alonzo Springstead of Geneva to build a second boat. Benjamin had built the *Joseph Wood*. The plan for Captain Wood was to have two steamers operating on the lake, but that was not to be.

Four months after Wood bought the *Steuben*, it burned at the dock in Penn Yan. The August 11, 1864 issue of the *Yates County Chronicle* described the disaster:

> *Steamboat Burned—The steamer* Steuben, *which has plied so long on Crooked Lake, formerly under the command of Capt. Gregg and this year under Capt. Wood, was destroyed by fire at an early hour last Saturday morning. The fire must have originated before two o'clock and the boat was soon in flames. The Fireman and Engineer, who slept on board, escaped without their clothing and just in time. The first alarm was given by William Pruner and he made repeated calls before they were awakened.*

The firemen were very promptly on the ground and did splendid execution. But for their efforts, the boat would have burned to the water's edge. But the fire was extinguished, leaving the hull considerable charred but not consumed. We understand that boat was insured for $1800, probably $1000 less than its value. The boat can hardly be spared this season and we understand Capt. Wood will make an effort to secure a tug for the fall towing and such other business as it may suffice to do. He will proceed as fast as possible in the construction of a new boat, which will doubtless be in readiness for the season of 1865.

Construction on the new boat was indeed accelerated, as work started that November at a lumberyard along the lake outlet in Penn Yan and continued throughout the winter. For a little more than a year, the lake was without a steamer. In September 1865, the new boat was put into service. Since one of the major financiers of the project was Penn Yan businessman George R. Youngs, who was also a friend of Captain Wood's, the boat was christened the *George R. Youngs*. It was a 130-foot-long side-wheeler and, as the *Steuben* had done, carried passengers in the summer and agricultural products during the fall harvest, as well as towed canalboats and rafts of lumber.

Chapter 2

THE GOLDEN AGE OF STEAM

(1865–1915)

In the years following the end of the Civil War, there were a number of changes occurring around Lake Keuka, and in American society in general, that led to the rapid expansion of the steamboat business. One new development was the growth of grape farming and wine production. The first grapes grown around Keuka Lake were grown by William W. Bostwick, a minister in Hammondsport, around 1830 to make sacramental wine for his church services. The vines he planted did extremely well; the soil and climate-moderating influence of the lake were a perfect combination. Soon Reverend Bostwick's neighbors were taking cuttings and planting their own small vineyards. Grape growing gradually spread northward from Steuben County into Yates County. By 1860, there were more than two hundred acres of vineyards around Keuka. Most of those were table grapes: Isabellas, Catawbas, Concords, Delawares and Niagaras. The first winery in the Finger Lakes, the Pleasant Valley Winery (also known as the Great Western Winery), opened in 1860 two miles south of Hammondsport. Using French winemakers, it turned out its first wine in 1862. The Urbana Wine Company, which later became Gold Seal, opened a few years later in 1865 and the Taylor Winery in 1880. By 1900, there were forty wineries in the area.

Early roads around Lake Keuka did not run parallel to the shoreline. They came straight down the hills from the farms to the lake. During the grape harvest, area farmers brought their wagonloads of grapes down to the packinghouses and docks around the lake to be loaded onto one of the steamboats. Lake Keuka grapes and wine built quite a reputation around the

Northeast, and the Crooked Lake Canal provided access to wider markets, especially New York City. The canal, however, was becoming a problem in the late 1860s and early 1870s. The cost of maintaining and repairing an eight-mile canal with twenty-eight locks resulted in over forty years without making a profit. Railroad expansion across the state meant lost canal business and revenues. For example, in 1871, it cost the canal operators $673 to collect $301 in tolls. It caused the *Yates County Chronicle* to ask, "What sane man would think of continuing business at such a ruinous sacrifice?"[1] New York State considered abandoning the canal (which it did in 1877), while area farmers and businessmen looked to the railroads.

The Civil War had proven how vital a railroad network could be as the Union army could readily and rapidly move troops and supplies into Virginia and Tennessee. That plus the disruption of Southern railroad lines was an important factor in the ultimate victory. After the war, the entire nation experienced a period of "railroad fever." The first transcontinental railroad to the Pacific was completed in 1869, and plans were made for others to be built. Progressive small towns across the county realized that their future growth depended on a railroad connection. Penn Yan had had railroad service since the 1850s with the Canandaigua and Elmira road (later the Northern Central), but there was a need for expanded service directly to the lake. In 1872, the Bath & Hammondsport (B&H) Railroad was chartered, and construction was begun on the nine-mile narrow-gauge line that connected the two villages and provided Keuka Lake with access to the Erie Railroad system. By 1875, the line was completed and a terminal and warehouses were built right on the Keuka waterfront in Hammondsport.

Even before the Crooked Lake Canal was abandoned by the state in 1877, there was talk among Penn Yan businessmen and area farmers of another railroad connection. There was general concern over the rates and policies of the Northern Central and fear that neighboring communities would acquire connections and leave Penn Yan as a backwater. There was serious consideration given to a railroad running up the east side of Lake Keuka from Corning, the Sodus Bay and Corning Railroad, but there were financing and right of way problems with that route. The *Yates County Chronicle* complained:

> *Penn Yan in its younger days had an eye to business, when it dug its canal that gave it a lift ahead of all its rivals as a shipping port and business center. With its public interests thus jealously watched, our village has rapidly grown and today stands without a business rival in the State for a place of*

its size. How shall it hold its present supremacy is a question demanding the immediate attention of its men of business. Our neighboring rivals were never as active as at present in seeking to cut off our trade, one by a railroad through Hall's Corners, Potter Center, Branchport and Hammondsport to Bath and the other by a road through Naples and Rushville to Bloods. Dundee also on the south is seeking to draw the Corning and Sodus road out of its direct line for its accommodation and to the great damage of the road and of our place. Will any of these roads be built? We feel assured that at least one will.

Do the businessmen of Penn Yan desire the road or will they fold their hands and cry "a little more sleep and a little more slumber" and awake some morning to find depots at Branchport, Potter Center and Rushville and one-third of their trade lost forever? Nothing will prevent the building of one of those roads west of us but immediate and vigorous prosecution of the proposed line through this place. The life blood of our village comes through its mills, factories and machine shops—its outstretching avenues of trade and ample railroad facilities. Let us see to it that these are not crippled, but fostered and multiplied; and our railroad, now under contract to this place, pushed along to an early completion.[2]

The same year that the canal was abandoned (1877), a railroad was built down the west side of Seneca Lake from Geneva to Watkins through the village of Dresden. The Syracuse, Geneva & Corning Railroad was part of the New York Central system. Community leaders started thinking about connecting to it by building a short line seven miles up the old canal towpath from Dresden to the Lake Keuka outlet in Penn Yan. The Penn Yan and New York Railway Company was formed in 1877, but the old towpath had to be acquired from the state and details had to be worked out with the connecting railroads. Finally, in 1885, the first trains came up from Dresden on what was called the Fall Brook Railroad. That meant that Keuka Lake was then connected to the Pennsylvania, New York Central and Erie Railroad systems.

A third factor in creating the golden age of steam on Lake Keuka was the rapidly expanding economy. Westward expansion, increased industrialization and urbanization created a very wealthy class of businessmen with surplus capital to invest, but it also led to the growth of the middle class. It is said about the economy that "a rising tide lifts all boats," and one can take that phrase literally, as it certainly benefited the steamboat trade on Lake Keuka. Summers and new affluence brought thousands of what then were called "excursionists" to the lake from throughout the Northeast. They took the

B&H Railroad to Hammondsport or the Northern Central or Fall Brook to Penn Yan, boarded one of the steamers and made their way to one of the many resorts that were being built along the shoreline. Summer homes, called "cottages" on Keuka, were being built by those with the means to do that. Some of the excursionists rented cottages by the week or month. Many stayed in hotels in either Penn Yan or Hammondsport and took day trips out on the lake, often being dropped off at one of the docks along the lake for picnics, fishing or swimming.

In addition to the excursionists, a large part of the steamboat business came from people who lived locally. For example, people from Pulteney would board a boat at Gibson's on the west branch and go to Penn Yan for a day of shopping or to see a doctor. After 1890, assemblies or chautauquas at Keuka College provided business opportunities. Community groups (churches, schools, veterans, fraternal organizations) would charter boats for excursions. Many locals simply enjoyed being out on the lake during good weather—a day of fishing perhaps, or a swim on a hot day. There were scheduled stops at some landings along the lake, but there were also "flag stops" where people would put a white flag out on the end of the dock, providing a signal to the captain of a passing steamer to stop. They had to be aware, however, of the schedule of the last boat of the day. If they missed it, it was sometimes a long walk back to town through the farms, fields and woods, since there were no roads along the shoreline.

Chapter 3

THE STEAMBOAT WARS

(1872–1892)

O ne doesn't normally associate the peaceful waters of Keuka Lake with any kind of war, but as the steamboat era entered its golden age in the decades following the Civil War, there were three steamboat "wars." Each was actually a struggle for dominance between competing companies on the lake. This was the time when men in business and finance amassed large fortunes throughout the economy by using cutthroat competition to create monopolies. Steamboat companies on Keuka Lake did not escape that type of competition.

The decade of the 1870s began with Captain Allen Wood having a monopoly of service on the lake with his two boats, the *George R. Youngs* and the *Keuka* (II). He ran both boats once a day between Penn Yan and Hammondsport. Between the excursionists and the local farm traffic, he did quite well financially and began to think of other outlets for his money. Captain Wood started by buying vineyards on the southern end of the lake, but early in the decade, businessmen in Hammondsport started to talk about constructing a nine-mile narrow-gauge railroad from Bath to Hammondsport. That would connect the village and Keuka Lake to the Erie Railroad system and give a major boost to Wood's steamboat business. Captain Wood wasn't the only one to see that potential.

In the early years of the decade, Joseph Crosby, an early Lake Keuka grape farmer, formed a company to compete with Allen Wood: the J.F. Crosby Company. Crosby had considerable influence in Yates County, having served both as county supervisor and sheriff. The enterprise soon attracted

Morris Sheppard, whose interest in one of the steam boat companies led to the third "steamboat war."

the money and support of two Penn Yan businessmen, banker Morris Sheppard and Farley Holmes. Together they formed the Lake Keuka Navigation Company (LKNC) and hired Alonzo Springstead to commence construction of a new steamer along the outlet in Penn Yan. Captain Wood, not relishing the idea of competition on the lake and wanting to get more involved with the railroad between Bath and Hammondsport, made an amicable deal with the new company in the fall of 1871. Two results of that arrangement were that the *G.R. Youngs* was sold to Crosby's company and Wood agreed that the *Keuka* (II) would not compete with the new company. For the 1872 season, Crosby's company had both the *G.R. Youngs*—which was renamed the *Steuben*—and the brand-new boat, a 115-foot-long side-wheeler that was christened the *Yates*. The two boats gave Crosby's company what appeared to be a monopoly of service on the lake. From the *Yates County Chronicle* on November 30, 1871:

> *We learn that the steamboat company of which ex-Sheriff Crosby is the principle member, have purchased of Captain Wood the steamer* Youngs *and all his franchises on the lake consisting of docks, landing places, and other property. This consolidates the steamboat interest on the lake and with the new boat now in process of construction by Mr. Springstead at the stave yard in this village, Commodore Crosby will open the next summer campaign under the most favorable auspices. Capt. Wood has built up a*

fine business on the lake and, under the new company the business cannot fail to be largely increased by reason of the added and elegant facilities the new company will offer. We congratulate the Commodore on the prospects of success which attend his steamboating enterprise.

Allen Wood used the money from the sale of the *Youngs* to invest heavily in the construction of the railroad. He decided to sell the *Keuka* (II) to Archibald Thayer, who promptly renamed it the *Stranger* and went into competition with the new company. Crosby's company considered that a breach of contract in its agreement with Captain Wood. Thus began the first of three steamboat "wars" in the late nineteenth century, although this one was little more than a skirmish. Thayer relished the competition, but Wood didn't. Lawsuits would be drawn out and expensive, so Wood got Thayer to sell him back the boat. (They had been partners in the past.) Archibald Thayer then started making plans to build another boat for the Keuka trade. Crosby's company headed that off by making Thayer a lucrative offer to join the company as captain of the *Steuben*. Thus ended the 1873 "war" and restored a monopoly to the Lake Keuka Navigation Company. The company's slogan: "Two boats a day, each way, will be the order of the day."

The following is from the *Yates County Chronicle* in August 1873:

Lake Keuka—Our beautiful Keuka will yet inspire the song of the poet as few Lakes have, either in this country or in Europe. It is only just beginning to be appreciated by those residing near its picturesque shores. Tourists who have viewed the grand scenery of Switzerland, Italy, France, and other European countries, are most lavish in their praise of our own Lake Keuka scenery. The visitors from the cities of different States to this lake as a summer resort are largely increasing every year, and the indications are that its attractiveness will be enjoyed the coming summer by a far greater number of pleasure seekers than ever before. We hope to see multitudes come from all parts of the country, for the hotel accommodations in this village and at Grove Spring will surpass all previous seasons, and the Lake Keuka Steam Navigation Company are much better prepared to make it pleasant for all who ride on their fine steamers than they were last year, the high water enabling them to run their boats to the dock at the foot of Pine Street. The Steuben *has been dressed in handsome colors by artistic painters and starts out for business in elegant trim. The new steamer* Yates *which was built last year is to be repainted and tastily furnished. She will be ready for service as soon as the season for travel is fully open. Visitors to the Watkins*

Glen cannot afford to miss a ride over Keuka on one of the company's handsome steamers, and a view of the majestic hills and fruitful vineyards about Hammondsport and we certainly think none of them will fail to visit our Lake.

Crosby and Holmes's company was generally Penn Yan oriented and based its schedule on the arrival of trains on the Northern Central Railroad. In the summer of 1875, the Bath & Hammondsport Railroad was completed, and rail service began to the southern end of the lake. With the closing of the Crooked Lake Canal on the Penn Yan end and the completion of the B&H Railroad, businessmen in Hammondsport, led by Captain Allen Wood and George A. Sanders, sensed an opportunity and formed the Keuka Steamboat Company in 1877. This new company was to be Hammondsport oriented and coordinate with the schedule of the new railroad. They hired Alonzo Springstead to come to Hammondsport and build a steamboat near the new railroad at the foot of the lake. The new boat was launched in the spring of 1878 and was named *Lulu* after Lulu Sanders Mott, the daughter of George Sanders who later ran a very popular boardinghouse in Hammondsport. *Lulu* was only seventy-five feet long, and the new company lured Archie Thayer away from the old company to captain the new boat. *Lulu* was based in Branchport on the west branch of the lake, made connections with the B&H Railroad in Hammondsport and had docking rights in Penn Yan. Sanders's company also had plans in the works to build a bigger and faster boat.

So began the second "steamboat war." This one was a bit longer than the first and quite a bit nastier. Farley Holmes's company even took an express wagon and team of horses down to Bath under the cover of darkness to be used to pick up passengers and freight that would otherwise have ridden on the B&H Railroad. The horse and wagon ride never caught on with the traveling public. They would rather ride a smooth railroad than a wagon on a bumpy road. It also helped that the railroad dropped its fares in order to compete. The nastiest event, however, occurred in August 1878. From the *Yates County Chronicle*:

STRANGE WICKEDNESS—Somebody moved by anything but honorable motives has twice attempted to sink the steamer Yates. On Friday evening two holes were bored through her sides below the water line and another attempted, but the augur struck an iron and the work was not completed. The boat filled with about three feet of water and careened toward the dock throwing the holes out of the water. She was pumped out and the holes were plugged and all was right again. On Saturday another attempt was made, but a watch being kept, Mr. James Conklin found a man in the wheel house who dropped his augur on being discovered and swam across the channel. Mr. Conklin fired twice at him, but there is no evidence that his shots had any effect. What could be the motive for so grave a crime is not easily comprehended.

Freight and passenger rates on the lake were slashed, and lawsuits went into court as competition between the two companies heated up. With newer, faster boats (*Lulu* and the *Urbana*) and a more predictable schedule, the Keuka Steamboat Company clearly became the line the public favored. Farley Holmes's company started to face financial problems that only worsened. In the fall of 1879, Farley Holmes became ill and died suddenly in early December at the age of fifty-seven. He had been using his own finances to keep the company going. In 1880, a bad storm coming up the lake severely damaged the *Steuben*. With debts piling up, the two boats of the old Lake Keuka Navigation Company were sold to the new company in January 1881. The old company disbanded, thus ending the second "boat war."

Allen Wood, George Sanders and their Keuka Steamboat Company then enjoyed a monopoly of service with the large boats. They reorganized as the Lake Keuka Navigation Company and broadened

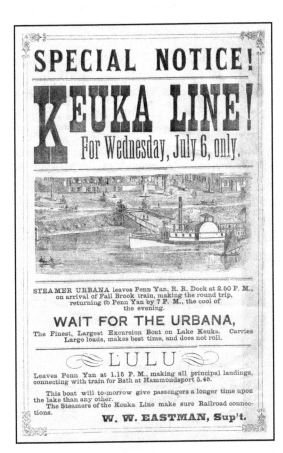

Keuka Line excursion poster, circa 1885, featuring connections to the railroad in Penn Yan and Hammondsport for day trips.

their financial support by taking in a few Penn Yan businessmen in the leadership—namely, Ralph Wood and Morris Sheppard. They had three large boats: *Lulu*, *Yates* and the *Urbana*. The *Steuben* had been badly damaged in the storm the year before and was towed down to Hammondsport to be taken out of service. Freight rates and ticket prices were raised in order to make up for cuts that had been made as a result of the earlier competition. Their monopoly didn't last long.

Into this scene came William L. Halsey. Halsey was born and raised in Steuben County but went west as a young man and made his fortune in railroads and steamboats in the Pacific Northwest. (There is a town in Oregon named after him.) He returned to New York in the 1870s and lived in Rochester. There he got involved in various business enterprises and a law practice, all of which added to his wealth. He bought land on Keuka Lake and built a large cottage near the Grove Springs Hotel named Care Naught. There he developed a friendship with Farley Holmes and, because of that, closely followed the second "boat war" of 1878–81. Troubled by the shabby treatment of Holmes's widow by the new company, Halsey started buying stock in the Lake Keuka Navigation Company and won a seat on its board of directors. As the story goes, he was incensed one stormy night in 1882 when the *Urbana* refused to stop at his dock at Care Naught. Days later, he confronted Morris Sheppard (who by then was an officer in the company) on Main Street in Penn Yan, saying, "If you can't operate this boat to accommodate the public, I'll build one of my own!" Sheppard's response was, "You couldn't build a rowboat!" That started the third and final "steamboat war."

Halsey allied himself with some powerful Penn Yan businessmen: Theodore O. Hamlin, who ran the Metropolitan,

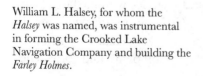

William L. Halsey, for whom the *Halsey* was named, was instrumental in forming the Crooked Lake Navigation Company and building the *Farley Holmes*.

Theodore O. Hamlin, more commonly known as "T.O.," was involved in the management of steamboat companies and owned a major dry goods store in Penn Yan.

a dry goods store on Main Street; Oliver C. Knapp, who ran a downtown hotel; and William Wise of Hollowell & Wise Hardware. They formed the Crooked Lake Navigation Company and hired Alonzo Springstead to build an elegant state-of-the-art steamboat, the *Farley Holmes*, which Halsey named after his friend. The competition started in earnest when the *Holmes* was launched at Hammondsport in July 1883. The maiden voyage included guests personally invited by Halsey. A special dinner was held at the Grove Springs Hotel, and then the *Holmes* proceeded north to enter the outlet and dock at Penn Yan. The "new line" (Halsey's company) had leased a dock near the steamboat landings, but there were rumors that there might be a confrontation with workers from the "old line." The county sheriff was on hand with twenty-five deputies in case they were needed. A large crowd gathered on both sides of the outlet to see the new boat and watch what happened as it tried to dock. The *Holmes*'s dock had one of the "old line" boats tied up to it, but it was removed without incident, according to this story in the *Penn Yan Express* on July 18, 1883:

THE NEW STEAMER—The new steamer "Farley Holmes" made her first appearance in Penn Yan on Saturday last. She had on board a party from Rochester and arrived at the dock in this village about half past twelve o'clock. Her arrival was witnessed by a large crowd of people and in attempting to make a landing a little unpleasantness occurred which has been the occasion of a good deal of unnecessary excitement and wild talk. It seems that there is a dispute in regard to the title to the dock which extends out into the outlet. The Keuka Navigation Company have had peaceful occupation of the dock for some time and claim that they have a legal title to the same. The new company denies this and contends that it possesses the title. On the arrival of the Farley Holmes, the officers of the old company undertook to maintain their possession of the dock, but at the same time offered the new company the privilege of landing by the side of their boat or at another dock owned by them which was then unoccupied. Urged by the crowd and Under Sheriff Swarthout assisted by twenty-five deputies (who claimed the right to enforce an injunction which had been issued by Justice James C. Smith commanding the old company to permit the landing of the boat of the new company at their dock) the new company decided to take forcible possession of the dock and succeeded in their effort.

According to Theodore Hamlin, secretary of the new company:

Oliver C. Knapp was Superintendent of our company and was on the end of the pier, and when the Holmes came he signaled to come head on slowly to the end of the pier. The Holmes did so and poked its bow between the Yates and the pier, the hawser holding the Yates getting over the bow of the Holmes. Mr. Halsey on the Holmes called for an axe and cut the hawser and the Holmes pushed the Yates away and landed at the pier. To provide for a landing at night on returning, Superintendent Knapp had a canal boat tied at the pier until the Holmes came down. He afterwards told me that bloodshed had been threatened, if necessary, to prevent the landing of the Holmes. Personal conflicts were narrowly averted and altogether it was a very exciting episode. When the Holmes affected a landing, the crowd on the bank gave a cheer and we then knew they were our friends.[3]

The competition that started at that point lasted for nine years. On one side was the "old line" (the Lake Keuka Navigation Company), with its flagship the *Urbana* mainly backed by Hammondsport business interests and, thanks to the Bath & Hammondsport Railroad, business interests in Corning and Elmira. On the other side was Halsey's new company (the Crooked Lake Navigation Company), with its flagship the *Holmes* backed by Penn Yan business interests and, thanks to the North Central Railroad, business interests in Rochester and Buffalo. When William Halsey suddenly died in 1884, the company was taken over by his wife and T.O. Hamlin. They built one of the longest steamboats yet seen on the lake and named it the *William L. Halsey* when it was launched at Penn Yan in 1887. This allowed them, with the *Holmes* and the *Halsey*, to double-team the old line on the regular run between Penn Yan and Hammondsport. For nine years, there were lawsuits and injunctions, competition over docking rights and price slashing. Boats of the opposing lines raced one another to the docks to pick up the passengers first, resulting in a few collisions. Local newspapers got involved in what was referred to as "The Steamboat Unpleasantness." The *Penn Yan Express* of July 18, 1883, cautioned the people to let the issue be settled in the courts between the two companies: "In the meantime, right-minded people will endeavor to quiet the unwarranted excitement and to treat the steamboat companies in accordance with their merits. Legitimate opposition is all right; it benefits the people and affords them protection against monopoly; but opposition founded upon spite and having no higher inspiration than damage or ruin to the object of its malevolence should be frowned upon by all good people." The *Penn Yan Democrat* saw it differently and accused the *Express* of siding with the old company. The *Express* responded, "To the charge of the *Democrat* that we are defending an oligarchy that seeks to rule in all matters, we only desire to remark that in our opinion the managers of the Keuka Company are no more vulnerable to unfavorable criticism than those of the new line which it defends with such vigor."

The main beneficiary of this competition was the public, as the price of a ticket went from $1.50 down to $0.10 one way to anyplace on the lake. The tension of 1883 and 1884 diminished somewhat in the years that followed, although it didn't disappear entirely. The two companies even cooperated at times. Fred Maxfield, who worked on the *Urbana* and other boats during the era, later said, "You'd think the men on the different lines were bitterest enemies, as they raced to be first at the different docks and used spy glasses to count the passengers at different points and decide which dock was worth tying up to. But when the day was over, they'd settle down and have grand times together."[4]

With newer and more stylish boats, the "new line" held quite an advantage over the competition. However, both companies still made huge profits as the volume of business increased dramatically on Lake Keuka. This attracted the attention of a New York City businessman, Charles W. Drake, who was backed by other financiers. Drake had earlier been involved in railroads in the West. He started by buying the Bath & Hammondsport Railroad and the "old line" (the Lake Keuka Navigation Company) in 1890. He then set his sights on Mrs. Halsey, T.O. Hamlin and the "new line" (Crooked Lake Navigation Company). Rumors that Drake was going to have a steel-hulled boat built that would be the largest and finest on the lake, plus a purchase offer she couldn't refuse, caused Mrs.

Care Naught, north of Grove Springs, was the home of William Halsey later purchased by Charles Drake.

Halsey to sell her company and its boats to Drake in January 1892, thus ending the last of the "steamboat wars."

Charles Drake owned the steamboat line until he sold it to the Erie Railroad in 1904. During those twelve years, he spent his summers on the lake. He bought Care Naught, the cottage located near Grove Springs that had earlier belonged to William Halsey. He also bought Gleason's Point, located where the southern branch of the lake joins the east branch. It was named after Hiram Gleason, who ran one of the ferry services on the lake before the age of steam. Drake renamed it for his wife, Mary, and his daughter Lena. Thus, it became known as Marlena Point.

> *The steamboat service of Lake Keuka is far-famed. The entire trip of 22 miles costs but ten cents, making it without exception, the cheapest as well as the most delightful ride of America. The precipitous side of the lake are for miles covered with vineyards, farm-houses and woodland glens; while the shores are dotted with handsome cottages and hotels, affording a panorama of unceasing beauty and interest to the tourist when viewed from the deck of the passing steamer. On account of a strong competition*

Spirited Rivals, a 2002 painting by William F. Hopkins showing the flagships *Holmes* and *Urbana* racing down the east branch of the lake. *Used with permission of Carolyn Hopkins, the artist's widow.*

between the two Navigation Companies for several years past, the steamboat service is, without exception, far superior to any other upon the inland lakes. In speed, beauty, and elegance the boats are without rival for their size, while each boat adds to the delight of the tourist by furnishing an orchestra which discourses delightful music. The bustling activity of 1890 presents a strange contrast to the scenes of years ago when the fare for the trip was one dollar and the time of going the length of the lake was three or four times as long as now.[5]

Chapter 4

THE KEUKA STEAMERS

Note: When Roman numerals appear in parentheses along with a boat's name, keep in mind that they are only being used in this book to differentiate between boats of the same name. They were not actually used as part of the name at that time. For example, through the eighty years of the steamboat era, there were three boats named *Steuben*, two named *Keuka* and two named *Yates*.

THE *KEUKA* (1835–48)

The first steamboat on the lake was the *Keuka*, built in Hammondsport by the Crooked Lake Steamboat Company. The builder was Rumsey & Company of Geneva. It had a catamaran design with two eighty-foot-long Dunham boats as pontoons and a central paddle wheel. With a small wood-burning boiler, it was slow by later standards. Although the *Keuka* carried passengers (the fare: "eight shillings") and hosted a few social occasions, such as dances, it was mainly used to tow strings of canalboats to and from the recently completed Crooked Lake Canal in Penn Yan. The boat's first captain was Joseph Lewis of Geneva, who had captained boats on Seneca Lake. The engineer was John Gregg, who took over as captain in 1841. The boat made one trip a day between Hammondsport and Penn Yan.

From the Penn Yan Democrat of April 1839:

KEUKA

After undergoing thorough repairs will commence her regular trips on Monday the 15th inst., leaving Hammondsport at 4 o'clock a.m. on the arrival of the stage from Bath, intersecting at Penn Yan the stage for Geneva and Canandaigua, and arriving in Geneva in time for the stage or packet boats going east at 1 p.m. Returning, leaves Penn Yan at half past one p.m. on the arrival of the Geneva and Canandaigua stage. The stage from the boat the following line of stages: Dansville & Rochester, Olean & James Town, Painted Post & Elmira, and Harrisburg & Philadelphia.
Passengers by this line will reach Painted Post 8 hours sooner than by any other public conveyance.

Horses and carriages will be taken on board at either end of the lake.

J.S. Lewis, Captain

Above: This drawing of the first *Keuka* by artist Ross Plaisted shows canalboats being towed on the lake. He made his drawing from descriptions of the boat, as no photos or other drawings are known to exist.

Left: This 1839 news article describes the boat meeting the stagecoaches as later boats timed their schedules to meet the trains.

One dark night in 1848, the pilot (allegedly intoxicated) lost his bearings and missed the dock in Hammondsport. He instead ran the boat up into the inlet, where it struck a sunken log and suffered severe damage. Calvin Carpenter of Penn Yan bought the wreck for twenty-five dollars and scrapped parts of it. The main cabins, however, were hoisted onto a flat barge and towed down to the Penn Yan end of the lake, where it was eventually moored near a sulphur spring along the eastern shoreline, about a mile from the end of the lake. His wife made the comment that it looked like Noah's ark, and the name stuck (more about the Ark in Chapter 5).

THE *STEUBEN* (1845–64)

A few years before the *Keuka* met its untimely end, a group of Hammondsport businessmen made plans to form a company and build a larger, faster and more stylish boat. They brought a boat builder up from New York City, and work was commenced at Hammondsport in the fall of 1844. The launching took place in June 1845, and the boat was christened the *Steuben*. John Gregg came over from the *Keuka* and became the first captain of the *Steuben*, eventually becoming the owner. For many years, the *Steuben* was the only steamer on the lake. It was a 126-foot-long side-wheeler and, like the *Keuka*, was primarily used for towing canalboats and rafts of logs. However, Captain Gregg put more emphasis on passenger traffic and excursions. The captain, born in Ireland in 1811, was described as an affable host on the boat who catered to the public. As a result, the *Steuben* was quite a popular boat with the public.

In the spring of 1864, John Gregg, realizing that his boat was aging and having interests in the Pleasant Valley Winery near Hammondsport, decided to sell the *Steuben* to Allen Wood and buy vineyards on Bluff Point. The April 4, 1864 issue of the *Yates County Chronicle* reported, "Crooked Lake—Capt. J. Gregg, who has commanded on Crooked Lake till he seemed to be chief proprietor of that sheet of water, has sold the steamer *Steuben* and all his prerogatives therewith connected to Capt. Allen Wood of Canandaigua." Unfortunately (as described earlier), Captain Wood's time with the *Steuben* was limited to four months, as the steamer caught fire at the dock in Penn Yan and was totally destroyed. That left the lake without steamer service for just over a year.

THE *GEORGE R. YOUNGS/STEUBEN* (II) (1865–79)

The old steamer Steuben was burned on the 9th of August last year. It has taken a little more than a year to supply its place with a new boat from which we trust much benefit will accrue to all interested in the navigation of one of the finest lakes in the world.[6]

Even before the burning of the *Steuben*, Allen Wood and his Lake Keuka Steamboat Line had plans to bring Benjamin Springstead over from Geneva to build a new boat. The demise of the *Steuben* just accelerated the schedule. Springstead commenced work along the outlet in Penn Yan in November 1864. Having suffered financially because of the *Steuben*, Captain Wood sought backing from his friends around the lake. One major benefactor was businessman George R. Youngs of Penn Yan, who had made his fortune in a variety of enterprises: stock speculation, Penn Yan's first malt house, the lumber business and banking. With that financial backing, Captain Wood commenced work on the boat in a lumberyard along the Keuka outlet in Penn Yan in November 1864. In May 1865, the new boat was ready to be launched and christened. The *Yates County Chronicle* of May 25 recorded the scene:

The *George R. Youngs* was built by Benjamin Springstead, father of Alonzo, who built most of the boats to later steam on Keuka's waters.

STEAMBOAT LAUNCH—*The new steamboat of Captain Allen Wood was launched last Saturday afternoon (May 20th.) About three o'clock a large gathering of people filled Bush's Lumber Yard, covered the Liberty Street bridge, and lined the bank on the opposite side of the outlet. At the appointed hour, the workmen knocked away the blocking which supported the boat and at the proper signal she slid gaily into the water, making a prodigious swell for a few moments which soon subsided, leaving the new boat sitting as gracefully as a bird on its destined element. The boat was named after our fellow citizen George R. Youngs who will no doubt respond handsomely in the fitting up of the cabin for the compliment. It is quite certain now that we shall soon have a boat worthy of our beautiful lake, if no unfortunate casualty intervenes and it will soon be a source of much profit and pleasure to all concerned. The launch was followed by brief speeches by Darius Ogden and Daniel Morris, the band played a few tunes, and the people dispersed well-pleased with the entertainment.*

The *G.R. Youngs*, a 130-foot side-wheeler, brought steamboat service back to the lake in September 1865. On its trial run from Penn Yan to Hammondsport on September 7, Captain Wood invited one hundred Penn Yan dignitaries—businessmen, politicians, newspaper editors and ministers. They were entertained on board by the Penn Yan Cornet Band. The boat was a bit slower than anticipated and reached the hotel in Hammondsport late into the dinner hour. The hotel in Hammondsport also was not prepared to serve one hundred people at once. It took two hours for everyone to be served, amid complaints of starvation. One of them, Editor Cleveland of the *Yates County Chronicle*, later wrote, "We trust the Hammondsport hotel will increase the power of accommodations for the future."

Adaptations were made to the boat to increase its speed, and it was soon ready for regular service. Although the *Youngs* did the usual towing of canalboats and handling of freight, Captain Wood focused on passenger service.

For this reason the new steamboat was built to a much higher standard than her predecessor. Her cabins were large open rooms with plenty of windows to let the light and air in. They were furnished with carpets, couches, tables, chairs and mirrors. The boat had a kitchen and would become the first great steamer on Keuka Lake to serve hot meals to its passengers. The steamer G.R. Youngs was crowned with a large stateroom cabin on her aft hurricane deck which special parties could rent for the day. The stateroom cabin had the best view of the lake, giving special groups a private spot away from the other passengers.[7]

In the fall of 1871, rather than face competition from Joseph Crosby and Farley Holmes's recently formed Lake Keuka Navigation Company, Allen Wood sold the *Youngs* to them. For the 1872 season, they renamed the boat the *Steuben* (II). It continued to see service until 1880, when the boat was severely damaged during a storm out on the lake. The damage was so severe that the *Steuben* was towed down the lake to Hammondsport and taken out of service.

THE *KEUKA* (II) (1867–74)

With the return of peace and relative prosperity in 1865 and with business booming on the *G.R. Youngs*, Captain Allen Wood decided to build a second boat for his Lake Keuka Steamboat Line. He hired Alonzo Springstead to build it, which he did at his boat yard in Geneva. The boat was short compared to others on the lake (sixty feet, later lengthened to seventy-five) and was the first to have a propeller rather than a paddle wheel. The shell

A drawing of the second *Keuka* by Ralph T. Hall. This was the only Keuka steamboat not built on the lake. It was removed from the lake by way of the Crooked Lake Canal.

of the boat was towed to Dresden on Seneca Lake and brought to Penn Yan via the Crooked Lake Canal. The boat was finished in the Keuka outlet and christened *Keuka* (II). Its time on the lake was very short-lived. Between Allen Wood wanting to get involved with the Bath & Hammondsport Railroad and competition from the company formed by Joseph Crosby and Farley Holmes, it got caught up in the first "steamboat war." Wood first sold the *Keuka* to Captain Archie Thayer, who renamed it the *Stranger*, and then Wood bought it back and agreed to take it off the lake to settle disputes with the new company. *Keuka/Stranger* was sold to a Captain Schofield from Rochester in 1874, and it ended up conducting service between Charlotte and Irondequoit Bay on Lake Ontario.

THE *YATES* (1872–83)

The *Yates* was the first boat to be built by the Lake Keuka Steam Navigation Company. Again, this was done by Alonzo Springstead of Geneva. The side-wheeler boat was 115 feet long with a 20-foot beam. The *Yates County Chronicle* reported on April 11, 1872:

> *NEW BOILER*—*The boiler for the new steamer* Yates, *weighing eight tons, was drawn from the railway station yesterday to the steamboat dock by nine pairs of horses and mules and it made vigorous drawing necessary even for that amount of horse power. The boiler was manufactured by Mr. Wm. B. Dunning of Geneva and looks like a good piece of work. We notice that the newspapers all around are saying good things of Lake Keuka and its new steamboat arrangements. That it may be a prosperous season for the steamboat folks is our earnest wish.*

Having already bought the *G.R. Youngs* and renamed it the *Steuben*, the company chose the name *Yates* to broaden its appeal on Lake Keuka. Its slogan became "Two boats a day, each way, will be the order of the day." Captain Archie Thayer was the popular captain of the *Yates*, and according to the *Chronicle*, "She runs like a bird on the wave and will prove a fast sailer and in all respects just the thing she was built for."

Although a very popular boat during its time on the lake, it had its share of mishaps. In July 1873, J. Ralph Norris, a twenty-three-year-old member of Penn Yan–based Hyatt's Cornet Band, which was playing on board the

The *Yates*, from a stereograph, is shown at Hammondsport.

Yates, threw a bucket on a rope into the lake to collect water, and the speed of the boat pulled him over the rail. The boat was off the end of Bluff Point bound for Grove Springs. The steamboat company sent small boats out to search for him that night and dragged the lake that next morning. They even tried using nitroglycerine to explode deep in the water to get the body to rise to the surface. It didn't work; the body was never recovered.

In the summer of 1878, there was a serious collision between the *Yates* and a large sailboat named the *Jolly*. Due to confusion over signals, the *Jolly* found itself in the path of the steamer. The collision threw those on the sailboat into the water. All were rescued, but the *Jolly* had to be towed to shore for repairs. Later that summer, perhaps as a result of the second "boat war," someone twice bored holes below the boat's waterline in attempts to sink it at the dock in Penn Yan.

The worst mishap, however, occurred in November 1883. From the *Penn Yan Express* of November 21, 1883:

BURNING OF THE STEAMER YATES—*On Thursday morning last, at about two o'clock, the people of this village were aroused by the alarm of fire and a light in the western portion of the village directed them to the old steamboat dock at the foot of Pine Street, where it was discovered the steamer* Yates *of the Keuka Navigation Co.'s line was enveloped in flame. The fire department was promptly on hand and the engine was soon playing a lively stream on the burning mass of timber, but to no purpose as entire destruction was inevitable. The* Yates *was moored to the dock at her accustomed landing where she had been lying unused for a number of days, although a fire had been started under her boiler the day before for the purpose of blowing it off and cleaning it out preparatory for winter. Just how the fire originated which destroyed her is a mystery, but it is supposed it caught from sparks or live coals dropping from the fire-box.*

The Yates *was built during the fall and winter of 1872–73 on the cooper shop lot near the Liberty Street bridge and was therefore in her eleventh year. She was modeled and built by Mr. Springstead of Geneva. No pains or expense were spared in her construction and it is said that nothing but "clear stuff" was used in the timber line above and below the hold. She was*

Darius A. Ogden, local lawyer and legislator, was often called on to address the crowd at the launching of a new steamboat.

HON. DARIUS A. OGDEN.

a model of neatness in her day and was regarded as a very staunch craft. Her engine was purchased of the Seneca Lake Steam Navigation Co. and formerly did service for them in the steamer S.T. Arnot. Her boiler was new and was built in the western part of the state. She was a fast sailer and would have been swifter had her boiler been of sufficient capacity for her engine. She was also classed as a boat seldom meeting with an accident.

She was launched during the spring of 1873, a large multitude assembling to see her take to the water, the Hon. D.A. Ogden being present among the throng and making a speech appropriate to the occasion. She was completed during the summer of that year at a cost of $18,000 and made her first trip through the lake on the 4th of July.

She will be greatly missed by the patrons of the company, although we understand a new and elegant craft will take her place. The exact amount of insurance on the Yates we have not ascertained, but understand that it will fall a long ways short of covering the loss.

Three boat houses were also burned and boat owners were very numerous on the night of the fire looking after their interests. Luckily, there was but very little wind at the time and with but little sharp work the fire was got under control.

THE *LULU* (1878–95)

The construction of *Lulu* in Hammondsport in 1878 was a major factor in starting the second "steamboat war." It was another boat built by Alonzo Springstead of Geneva, this time for the Hammondsport-based Keuka Steamboat Company of George Sanders and Archie Thayer. It was seventy-five feet in length with a thirteen-foot beam. It had enclosed paddle wheels on both sides with four-foot-high letters reading "LULU" on the covers. *Lulu* was expected to be able to carry up to two hundred passengers and twenty tons of freight. *Lulu* had a few engineering issues, at least in the beginning. For one thing, it was noisy. It was said that the exhaust from its engines could be heard farther away than its whistle. It was also slower than had been anticipated. The story was told that on a test run, company officials were so upset with the boat's performance that a fistfight broke out.

In spite of those mechanical issues, the boat was clearly built for the passenger trade. The *Steuben Farmer's Advocate* of May 19, 1878, reported:

The *Lulu* was named for Lulu Sanders Mott, daughter of one of the owners who ran a popular boardinghouse in Hammondsport.

"The cabin is finished in oiled chestnut and has ten elegant plate glass windows. It is furnished with a Brussels carpet, two couches, two mirrors, two marble top tables, rocker and parlor chairs. The inside of the boat is finished with chestnut and oak, and presents a very neat appearance."

Lulu was christened and launched in late March 1878. However, it didn't go into service until the end of May because more work was needed on its boiler. It was named after George Sanders's daughter, Lulu Sanders Mott, who later ran a popular boardinghouse in Hammondsport. The boat was based in Branchport, which was a very popular move in that community, and made connections with the Bath & Hammondsport Railroad in Hammondsport. The decision to run it between Hammondsport and Penn Yan led to the "steamboat war" with the older company. Adding to the tension was the fact that Archie Thayer had been lured away from the older company's *Steuben* (II) to become captain of the *Lulu*.

One of the few fatalities of the steamboat era occurred on board the *Lulu* in December 1892. While the boat was near the Idlewild Hotel on the east branch, steaming toward the end of Bluff Point, twenty-two-year-old deckhand Eugene Robinson was throwing a bucket of ashes off the back of the boat. He slipped on ice and fell into the lake. With a heavy winter overcoat on, he went under the water very quickly. His body was never recovered.

The year 1895 was the last one in which *Lulu* saw service on the lake. Being the oldest boat in the fleet of Charles Drake's company and constantly in need of repair, it was towed back to Hammondsport and scrapped.

THE *URBANA* (1880–1904)

One would have to travel a good many miles before he could see a handsomer boat than the steamer Urbana. *Her model is one of the finest for the size we have ever seen and the manner in which she has been painted this season gives to her a very handsome appearance indeed.*[8]

The *Urbana* was built in Hammondsport during the winter of 1879–80 by Alonzo Springstead for the Hammondsport-based Keuka Steamboat Company of George Sanders and Allen Wood. It was launched in June

The *Urbana* at the Hammondsport docks. The railroad tracks in the foreground illustrate the importance of their proximity to allow for easy trans-loading.

1880 and put into service within a month. Its first captain was Archie Thayer (his fourth boat), and the pilot was Frank Conklin. It was a 120-foot-long side-wheeler with a 20-foot beam and destined to become the flagship of the company. *Urbana* was the fastest boat on the lake, having once made the twenty-two-mile trip from Hammondsport to Penn Yan in one hour and twenty minutes—including ten stops. The company's plan was for the *Urbana* to handle the passenger traffic while *Lulu* handled freight. *Urbana* was scheduled to meet the B&H Railroad in Hammondsport and the Northern Central in Penn Yan.

A distinctive feature on the *Urbana* was a metal figure of a deer that was put on its walking beam. When the boat was underway, the action of the walking beam made it appear as if the deer were running. It fascinated passengers on the boat as well as those on shore who watched the *Urbana* go past.

Its construction was a major factor ending the second "boat war" (1878–81) and, two years later, was a major factor in starting the third one (1883–92) when Captain Thayer refused to pick up William Halsey at his dock. *Urbana* had some serious mechanical issues during the first season of that "war," and Halsey's company spread the rumor that it had been pushed beyond its limits to keep up with the *Farley Holmes*—a rumor that the company (now reorganized as the Lake Keuka Navigation Company) flatly denied. There were numerous incidents of the *Urbana* racing the *Holmes* and later the *Halsey* racing to get to private docks first. There was a collision in the outlet in Penn Yan as the *Urbana* and the *Holmes* raced to the landing to pick up passengers at the steamboat dock.

The *Holmes* was a bit slower than the *Urbana*, but after William Halsey's death in 1884, his company made plans to build a new boat that would have the speed to compete. As that boat (which became the *Halsey*) was under construction in Penn Yan, the *Urbana* was overhauled at Hammondsport to prepare for the competition. The competition between the two companies abated somewhat in the late 1880s as the number of excursionists increased dramatically and both companies made substantial profits. That was what attracted the group of New York City financiers led by Charles W. Drake, who bought William Halsey's old cottage, Care Naught, in 1886 and then bought the Bath & Hammondsport Railroad. His next step in 1890 was to buy the Lake Keuka Navigation Company, which included the *Urbana* and *Lulu*.

By the early 1900s, the *Urbana* was starting to show its age and developed more and more mechanical issues. With newer boats in Drake's fleet, especially the *Mary Bell*, the *Urbana* was relegated to just freight in the 1903 season and was not in service at all in 1904. As Drake's Lake Keuka

The *Urbana* with a proud fisherman in the foreground showing his catch.

Navigation Company was negotiating with the Erie Railroad to purchase all his interests on Lake Keuka, the decision was made to have the *Urbana* towed to Hammondsport. It sank at the dock there in September 1904, and although there was talk of having it repaired in dry dock, the decision was made to dismantle it a month later.

THE *FARLEY HOLMES/YATES* (II) (1883–1915)

This was the first entry of William Halsey's Crooked Lake Navigation Company into the Lake Keuka steamboat business. The boat was built by Alonzo Springstead at Hammondsport, the fifth one he had built on Keuka since 1867. He had so much work in Hammondsport at that time—not just building boats but also repairing them—that he took up residence there between 1881 and 1883. He started this one in the spring of 1883, and it was completed in four months.

This boat was a 120-foot side-wheeler with a 20-foot beam and a capacity of 650 passengers. It was built to compete with the *Urbana*, which was the same size. According to the company's secretary, Theodore O. Hamlin, the boat "had special features entirely new on Lake Keuka. The upper deck

The *Farley Holmes*, later renamed the second *Yates*, operated on the lake for over thirty years.

was extended to the bow, adding largely to the carrying capacity, as well as furnishing an additional pleasant location for passengers. It also sheltered freight and passengers on the main deck below. Four or five hundred folding chairs were provided so that every passenger could have a seat except on special large occasions. Everything about the boat was new from stem to stern, which could not be said of any other steamer ever on the lake."[9]

Halsey named the boat after his good friend Farley Holmes, and the launching was in May 1883.

A large crowd of spectators had gathered to witness the event. Miss Kate Holmes of Penn Yan, the daughter of Farley Holmes, was given the honor of christening the boat with a bottle of champagne as the boat glided into the water. A fine orchestra of eight pieces from Penn Yan furnished music worthy of the notable event. About 150 people were on the deck when the boat was launched and some were considerable shaken up when the craft struck the water, the bow a little in advance of the stern, giving it a twisting motion. When they regained their footing and realized they weren't hurt, they gave three cheers for the Farley Holmes *and three more for Mr. Halsey.*[10]

The first excursion on July 14 led to the third and final steamboat "war." Halsey had invited a large group of friends from Rochester, Penn Yan and Hammondsport to go on the maiden voyage. The plan was to steam up the lake to Penn Yan to pick up more guests and then back south for a meal at the Grove Springs Hotel. Rumors had spread that there was going to be a major confrontation with the company that at the time dominated the steamboat trade: the Lake Keuka Navigation Company. A result of the rumors was that over one thousand people were at the steamboat dock in Penn Yan. The old company had put two of its boats, the *Lulu* and the *Yates*, on either side of a dock that Halsey had leased. Perhaps because of the number of witnesses and keeping public relations in mind, the old company backed away from any kind of confrontation with the *Holmes*. After some shuffling around of boats, the new boat was allowed to dock. When it left for Grove Springs, a canalboat was put at the dock to hold the spot. While the whole docking issue was being fought out in the courts, Halsey's company leased and then bought land on the opposite (south) side of the outlet and put in its own dock.

The first captain of the *Holmes* was Oscar Morse, and Frank Morse was the pilot. The entire crew wore uniforms, which was a first for steamers on the lake. The first regular trip was on July 19, 1883. That day, the *Holmes* carried nearly six hundred passengers who paid ten cents to go to any point on the lake. The *Holmes* didn't operate on Sundays, in part for religious reasons but also to give the crew a day off and have minor repairs and cleaning done on the boat.

One of the popular attractions on the new *Holmes* was its candy stand, which received rave reviews in local newspapers. From the August 23, 1883 edition of the *Yates County Chronicle*:

> One of the greatest conveniences on the new line is the refreshment center run by Ed Quick. Ed knows how the candy business should be carried on and carries it on just in that way. It is very pleasant to the inner man and refreshing withal, to run across that corner of the steamer about six o'clock of a chilly evening, when the sun is thinking about going down behind Bluff Point and the aforesaid inner man is thinking of the flesh pots of Penn Yan. That is the exact season of the year when a sandwich tastes like one. Ed says he has a good trade—sold seventy-five sandwiches the first day, besides confectionary. Confectionary is a good article to sell on a steamer, for it can be disposed of there with good profit. Get a young fellow up in front of the stand with his girl by his side and he pays whatever price

is asked. He wouldn't beat down a cent for four dollars and he spends his last dime without a murmur. Talk about women's rights and women's influence! Great Scott, women's influence does more for the candy trade in the United States than all the glucose factories within its borders. Without it, the ice cream business would wither away like a hat feather in an August shower, and the clang of the freezer would be heard no more in the land.

In August 1888, the *Holmes* had passengers out on a moonlight cruise. After leaving Finton's Landing on the east branch, Pilot Frank Conklin realized the boat had somehow lost its rudder. By the time he realized it, they were out in the middle of the lake. The boat used its whistle to attract attention, but there was no response, so a deckhand set out in a lifeboat to summon assistance. By this time, the *Holmes* had drifted down near the Idlewild Hotel on Bluff Point. The deckhand reached the hotel, and the owner started up his steam yacht, the *Minnie V.*, and towed the *Holmes* to the dock at the Idlewild. The *Minnie V.* then went to Hammondsport and summoned the *Halsey* to come get the stranded passengers. By the time the *Halsey* got to Idlewild, it was daybreak. A small boy on board the *Holmes* had a large supply of peanuts and sold them to the hungry passengers until the hotel was ready to serve breakfast.

Although involved in a serious accident on the lake in 1897, the *Holmes* was an unusually reliable boat and quite popular with the public. Its peak year was 1886, when it carried over

Oscar Morse was an engineer, pilot and captain on numerous boats. The captain of a steamboat was the business manager; the pilot ran the boat.

sixty thousand passengers for the season. It was handed down through two more owners: the first time when Halsey's company sold it to Charles W. Drake in 1892 and again in 1904 when the Erie Railroad bought all of Drake's interests on the lake. The Erie management renamed the boat the *Yates* (II), and it stayed in service for ten more years. Finally, at the end of the 1915 season, the *Yates* was taken out of service. It was a thirty-two-year-old wooden-hulled steamboat, and the age and new technology had passed it by. It was towed to Hammondsport and dismantled. The empty hull was taken up the shore about two miles from Hammondsport on the west side and sunk. It eventually was filled with rocks and became part of a building lot.

THE *WEST BRANCH* (1883–1901)

This was the second boat built for William Halsey's Crooked Lake Navigation Company. As soon as work on the *Farley Holmes* was completed, Alonzo Springstead's crew went to work on this one. The *West Branch* was only sixty feet long with a twelve-foot beam and a propeller rather than a paddle wheel. Its cabin was fitted up with cherry wood trim, and it had an awning to cover the deck. It made its trial run on August 19, 1883, with local dignitaries on board and then was soon ready for regular service. It was intended to mainly carry freight but could also carry up to one hundred passengers. At the end of that first season, it had some labor problems, as the *Hammondsport Herald* reported in October: "Frank Conklin, captain of the steamer *West Branch*, Harry Morse the pilot, and Will Van Lew the engineer, with the fireman, severed their connection with the company last week—the captain on account of trouble with the Superintendent, Morse for higher wages, and the rest because the others did. Some of the places will be difficult to fill."

As its name would imply, this boat was built to challenge the *Lulu* on the west branch of the lake. It competed with *Lulu* but found it impossible to break the popularity that boat had with the people of Branchport and the farmers along the west branch of Lake Keuka. Although it made regular runs between Branchport and Gibson's Landing, it also ran the main line between Penn Yan and Hammondsport in connection with the *Holmes*. In running the main line, the *West Branch* found itself in competition with the *Yates*. A story in the *Penn Yan Express* described a race of sorts between the *Yates* and the *West Branch* after coming out of the outlet at Penn Yan. Branchport resident George Weaver had his steam yacht, the sixty-foot *Mascot*, at the Ark

Above: The *West Branch* operated primarily in the west branch of Keuka, hence its name. It was the first propeller-driven steamer on the lake.

Right: The *West Branch* shown passing Drake Point. This was a flag stop, meaning it had sufficient depth to accommodate the boats and was not a scheduled stop but the boat would land there if a white flag was put out.

near Penn Yan and joined in the race. The *West Branch* beat both boats as they raced down the east branch.

In 1890, when Charles Drake bought the B&H Railroad and the Lake Keuka Navigation Company (the old line), the Crooked Lake Navigation Company decided to upgrade the *West Branch* to prepare for renewed competition. Alonzo Springstead was called back to lengthen the boat by fifteen feet. After two seasons of intense competition, the boat was sold to Drake, along with all the other assets of William Halsey's old company.

The *West Branch* continued to see service through the 1900 season. In November of that year, while tied up at the dock in Hammondsport, the boat was battered by a fierce winter storm. The pounding broke a hole in it. It filled with water, broke in two and went to the floor of the lake. The *West Branch* stayed there through the winter of 1900–1 and was finally raised that spring and scrapped.

THE *WILLIAM L. HALSEY/STEUBEN* (III) (1887–1915)

After the death of William Halsey in 1884, his widow, Helen, and the company president, Theodore Hamlin, made the decisions for the Crooked Lake Navigation Company. One of the key decisions was to have a new boat built that could pair up with their other big steamer, the *Holmes*, and compete with the competition's flagship, the *Urbana*. Once again, Alonzo Springstead was lined up to build the boat at the foot of the lake near Penn Yan—his seventh Keuka steamer. The lumber for the boat came off land near Pulteney. This boat was the longest yet seen on Lake Keuka at 130 feet with a 22-foot beam. It was christened the *William L. Halsey* and made its first regular trip down the lake in June 1887.

Its first crew had Oscar Morse as captain, Frank Morse as pilot and John Long as engineer. As on the other boats of the Crooked Lake Navigation Company, the crew all wore uniforms. The *Halsey* could cruise the lake at twenty-two miles per hour. Its fastest time from Penn Yan to Hammondsport was about an hour and a half, including stops. In the summers, the *Halsey* made two trips a day on the lake, including nineteen stops each way. Ten cents got a passenger one way to any point on the lake.

The *Halsey* was very popular with the public. Its most impressive day was the Fourth of July 1888, when it carried over 2,300 paying passengers. One week in August of that year, it carried over 7,100 passengers. The Crooked

Above: The *William L. Halsey* leaving
Hammondsport was rated for 850 passengers,
and they all appear to be on board this day.
The bow of the *Holmes* can be seen behind
the *Halsey*.

Right: Helen Halsey, William
Halsey's widow, participated in the
management after his death.

Lake Navigation Company
was proud of the fact that,
during the five seasons it
owned the boat, it carried
over half a million passengers
without a single injury. T.O.
Hamlin gave credit for that to
the company's landing policy:
"Landings were not allowed until
the steamer was made fast and the
gang plank safely placed."[11]

This boat changed hands twice. The first
time was when Charles Drake bought out Mrs. Halsey's line before the
1892 season, creating a monopoly of steamboat service for his Lake Keuka

Navigation Company. The second time was in 1904, when Drake sold his company to the Erie Railroad. It promptly renamed the boat the *Steuben* (III).

The *Halsey* had its share of mishaps over the years, the most frightening of which happened in October 1897 when it collided off Bluff Point with the *Holmes*. From the *Yates County Chronicle*:

SERIOUS COLLISION ON THE LAKE—The Halsey *and* Holmes *Crash Together—Soon after six o'clock Thursday occurred the first serious accident to any of the steamboats on Lake Keuka. The* Halsey, *which all summer long has plowed the blue waters of the lake, was badly damaged by coming into collision with the* Holmes *near the end of Bluff Point.*

The story of the collision goes to show that all the trouble was caused by a misunderstanding of signals given by one boat, but just who was at fault we are not prepared to say. The Halsey, *which was on its way to Hammondsport, had made the landing at Keuka and was rounding the Point for Pulteney when the* Holmes, *on its way to Penn Yan from Pulteney, came around the Point from the west branch. The* Urbana, *which usually waits for the* Halsey's *Branchport customers at Gibson's had run over to the east branch to find whether the* Halsey *had any passengers aboard for her and finding she had none, turned about passing the* Holmes *in the west branch. The steamer* Cricket *was also in the west branch. The pilot of the* Halsey, *Mr. Frank Conklin, blew two blasts when he saw the* Holmes, *signaling that the boats pass each other on the left side, but the pilot of the* Holmes, *Mr. William Conklin, evidently thought the* Urbana *was the* Halsey *and that the signaling was for the* Cricket. *At any rate, he did not expect the* Halsey. *When the* Halsey's *pilot whistled again twice, the* Holmes *answered with one blast—the signal to go on the right side. Captain W.W. Eastman, who was aboard the* Holmes, *called the pilot's attention to the fact that he had not understood the signal. An attempt was then made to go to the left as signaled by the* Halsey. *The pilot of the* Halsey *by this time was changing the boat's course to follow the signal of the* Holmes. *These maneuvers brought the* Holmes *right athwart the* Halsey—*both boats were well loaded and going at full speed. As they came together, the* Halsey's *bow stem cut through the* Holmes' *side near the candy stand and smashed the woodwork along the upper deck and breaking her own bow stem and sampson-post off. The boats then sheared off. It was found that the* Halsey *was badly injured and the water was rushing into her hold*

The bow of the *Halsey* showing damage after its collision with the *Holmes*.

through the hole left by the broken bow stem. The boats were then about forty rods from the Bluff near Sturdevant's. The crews acted promptly and signals of distress were soon issuing, calling the Urbana *to their assistance. The* Holmes *and* Urbana *managed to run the* Halsey's *bow ashore before the water reached her fires.*

The collision, which came without the slightest warning, piled the passengers aboard the Holmes *in a heap near the railings and when they regained their feet, they imagined that the boat was going to sink, as they could not see the wrecked condition of the* Halsey. *They were remarkably cool, however, and with the exception of one man all showed courage in no small degree. This man, who was terror stricken, was held to prevent his jumping overboard. The passengers were transferred to the* Urbana *and taken to Hammondsport and later in the night the* Holmes *was able to make the run to the head of the lake. The* Halsey *had onboard about 6,000 baskets and 1,000 trays of grapes, which had been loaded at the landings along the lake and had aboard about fifteen passengers. She was taken to the dry dock in Hammondsport the following day. The* Halsey *was much the more seriously damaged, but just what the loss will be we cannot ascertain.*

There was a humorous side story to that collision that came out years later when national Prohibition went into effect. This letter to the *Yates County Chronicle* ran in a June 1920 issue. It was written by a regular letter contributor to the paper who lived on the lake and used the pen name "Hermit of the Lone Pine." In his letter, he described that 1897 collision between the two steamers and mentioned that two barrels of T.S. Burns's ale, brewed in Penn Yan, went to the bottom of the lake

> *brewed with honest skill of pure malt and the finest hops; aged and cared for as if it were priceless. Oh, cruel fate! At the first bump, the precious amber fluid, the nectar of the gods, slid gently overboard and fathoms deep it rested for years and years among the slimy ooze and cold eyed denizens of the lake. Then came the Great Drought. Wild eyed reformers won and a sore thirst pervaded the land. Prices of the drink that cheers and inebriates soared to realms before unknown.*

When Prohibition hit, two men who had witnessed the steamboat collision years earlier worked hard with surveyor's tools to locate the spot where the collision occurred. They got a crew together, including the "Hermit." In the winter, when the lake was frozen over, they located the spot and drilled a hole. Using chicken netting to capture the barrels, they left it in the lake until the ice went out in the spring. When they got the barrels on land, they decided to open one barrel and sample it. It had become quite concentrated and needed to be watered down. "Two of the party insisted on a drink of it 'straight.' They had it and started off home rowing with two sets of oars. The last we saw of them, they had each lost a port oar and were both pulling lustily on the starboard oar, going round and round like a duck with one

T.S. Burns was a local brewer and merchant. This is a label from his beer bottles.

leg trying to swim. One man was 44 hours reaching home, about two miles distant, and when he did get home his dog bit him and that dog had always known him too."

Another potential disaster was averted in November 1902, when the *Halsey* was caught out on the lake during hurricane-force winds. Loaded down with grapes toward the end of the harvest and passengers from communities around the lake who had been Christmas shopping in Penn Yan, it was heading south down the east branch of the lake, making its scheduled stops. A strong west wind increased dramatically in intensity, but with the shelter of Bluff Point, it had no problems until it cleared the end of the bluff and hit the wide waters. The boat had to make its usual stop at Keuka Landing since it had mail to deliver and passengers to let off. The waves were so rough that the boat couldn't tie up, and the wind and waves nearly grounded the *Halsey*. The captain decided to head over to the west side of the lake to Gibson's Landing to get into the lee of the hillside. Doing so headed the bow of the boat right into the waves, and the boat took a beating. A plank fell into the driving mechanism of the boat, and the captain had to stop the engine to determine the extent of any damage. The plank made a loud sound as it smashed into the walking beam, and that caused the passengers on board

This photo of the Hammondsport docks was taken from the hill on the west side of town. The large white building is the Fairchild House, a popular hotel.

to put on life jackets and wait for the order to abandon ship. However, the captain restarted the engine, and the boat made it to Gibson's. The trip from Keuka, which under normal circumstances took ten to twelve minutes, took an hour and fifteen minutes.[12] Staying along the western shore of the lake, the *Halsey* made its way to Hammondsport, where the company put up the undelivered passengers in the hotel for the night.

In the eighty years of the steamboat era, there were at least four fatalities; two of them occurred on this boat. The first one, in 1899, was when it was still the *Halsey*. The incident was described by the September 14, 1899 issue of the *Yates County Chronicle*:

> *FATAL ACCIDENT—On Thursday, John Bertholf of Elmira was killed while intoxicated by being struck by the connecting rod of the walking beam on the steamer* Halsey *and pushed through the hole in which this rod works to the hold below, as the boat was near Crosby on her up-trip in the morning. The body was transferred to the steamer* Holmes *and brought to the undertaking rooms of Corcoran Bros. in Penn Yan. Since the accident happened, hundreds of people have visited the steamer* Halsey *to see where the man met death. The hole through which Bertholf was crowded is only eight inches wide, and it seems almost impossible for a man's body to pass through this opening.*

The victim was twenty-nine years old. His friends testified that they left him sleeping in a chair and theorized that he was sleepwalking and went into the engine room. The second death was in August 1906:

> *FIREMAN KILLED ON LAKE—Edward Bert of Hammondsport was instantly killed yesterday morning on the steamer* Steuben *as that boat lay at her mooring in Hammondsport. Mr. Bert was fireman on the boat. Something was out of order with the machinery and in company with the engineer, Oscar Morse of Penn Yan, Mr. Bert went into the crank pit. The repairs having been made. Mr. Morse, supposing Mr. Bert had come out of the pit, started the engine. There is just about room enough in the crank pit when the walking beam descends to allow the shaft to turn, the result was Mr. Bert was literally crushed to death. His neck, back and arms were broken and otherwise terribly injured. Realizing something was wrong, Mr. Morse stopped the engine, but too late. Mr. Bert was twenty-two years old. About four years ago, when the* Steuben *was called the* Halsey, *a similar fatal accident occurred in the same crank pit. A passenger, more or less*

Oscar Morse is shown here in front of the engine of either the *Holmes* or the *Halsey*.

intoxicated, had someway opened the door leading into the pit. When the engine started, he was crushed.[13]

Another mishap occurred in August 1909. The *Steuben* had just left the dock at Keuka College when it collided with an anchored steam launch with two men fishing. The *Yates County Chronicle* reported that the pilot was outside the pilothouse signaling to friends on shore and wasn't watching where the boat was going. He had no idea that anything was wrong until the remains of the launch hit the paddle wheel of the *Steuben* and the boat came to a halt. Both the fishermen were pulled out of the lake and, although suffering from nervous exhaustion, were otherwise unhurt.

In late February 1911, the *Steuben* sank at the dock in Hammondsport, where it had been tied up for the winter. Employees had noticed that it was listing a few days earlier, but nobody did anything about it. It sank in about thirty feet of water and would have gone deeper had it not been tied up with strong hawsers. As many as thirty men went to work on raising the *Steuben*. A coffer dam was built around the boat, a diver went in to plug whatever holes there were and hydraulic pumps were used to get the water out of the boat. When it was raised and inspected, it was discovered that there was no

In 1911, the *Steuben* sunk at the dock at Hammondsport. It was floated, dried and returned to sail for another four years.

A girl on the dock sent this postcard image the next day describing the sinking of the *Steuben*.

damage to the boat. It was just that the company had not paid any attention to small leaks in the wooden hull and had not kept it pumped out. According to the *Hammondsport Herald*, "The story was that for three or four days before she sank, she sat very low in the water and tipped in toward the spiles. The morning that she sank, the wind changed and it is believed that when the boat tipped the other way she was setting so low that she immediately filled up through the ash hole."[14] The *Steuben* was soon repaired and ready for service again.

The *Steuben* made its last run in October 1915 when it was taken out of service and tied up at the dock in Hammondsport next to the already condemned *Yates*. It again sank at the dock in November 1916 and stayed there throughout 1917, much to the consternation of Theodore O. Hamlin, who wrote in November 1917: "Those who remember the service of this boat when operated by the Lake Keuka Navigation Company will learn with deep regret of her untimely end. She sank last winter while lying at her dock at Hammondsport and according to report, lies there in deep water and no effort made to salvage her fine engine." The fate of the *Steuben* was lost in local newspapers among war news, shortages, Liberty Bond drives and news of local men in the service "Over There" in Europe. The boat never was raised. Divers in 1960 located it in seventy feet of water off Hammondsport. They reported that there was still paint on some of the wood, and they could clearly make out one of the side wheels although it was buried in mud.

THE *MARY BELL/PENN YAN* (1892–1922)

Charles Drake brought an end to the final steamboat "war" by spreading rumors that he was going to have built the largest, most modern steamboat on the lake. It was enough to convince Mrs. Halsey and Theodore Hamlin to sell their Crooked Lake Navigation Company to Drake. It was more than just a rumor.

The *Mary Bell*, named after Charles Drake's wife, was built at Hammondsport by the Union Dry Dock Company of Buffalo and was quite different from any of the earlier boats on Keuka. At 150 feet, it was longer, it had a steel hull, it had twin propellers rather than a side wheel and it could cruise in excess of twenty miles per hour. In short, it was a state-of-the-art steamboat and was later described as "the finest boat on any inland waterway in New York." It cost between $45,000 and $50,000

The construction of the *Mary Bell* at Hammondsport in 1892 caused a lot of excitement.

The launching of the *Mary Bell* drew a crowd estimated by some to be forty thousand but was more likely in the five to ten thousand range.

to build, a tidy sum in those days. It had fine woodwork, brass fittings and up-to-date plumbing.

Assembled on the Hammondsport waterfront in the early spring of 1892, the boat was ready for launch in mid-May. Witnessed by a crowd estimated to be between five and ten thousand, speeches were given by Judge Hanford Struble of Penn Yan and other dignitaries. Then, bearing a bottle of Great Western Champagne adorned with red, white and blue ribbons, Mrs. H.S. Stebbins, wife of the manager of Drake's steamboat company, stepped forward and had the honor of christening the new boat: "I christen thee *Mary Bell*." After the bottle was smashed on the steel hull, the boat began to slide down the ways into the lake, accompanied by cheers and steamboat whistles. To the crowd's surprise (and amusement), the *Mary Bell* became stuck on the ways about halfway down. The band from the Soldier's Home in Bath, which had played at the ceremony, struck up "Dear, Dear, What Can the Matter Be?" The *Hammondsport Herald* of May 11, 1892, reported:

> The flight was retarded by the cooling of the heated grease and soft soap with which the ways were covered, in an unavoidable delay awaiting the arrival of the steamer Halsey, that her crowd of passengers might see the launching. Instead of rushing madly into the water as was anticipated, the handsome creature stuck on her timbers after having gone about half her length. It needed considerable persuasion to coax her from her resting place and finally, about 7:30, aided by the pulling of the Urbana and the vigorous working of jack screws at the bows, she slipped into the water, where she floats as gracefully as a swan.

After work on the interior was finished, it was ready for a trial run in mid-June. With one hundred invited guests on board, the *Mary Bell* left the waterfront at Hammondsport and made its way north up the lake toward Penn Yan. The *Hammondsport Herald* of June 22, 1892, reported, "As the *Mary Bell* gracefully steamed along, many manifestations of pleasure were observed from the residents along both shores. At the Ark a short stop was made where the new candidate for public admiration was witnessed, with exclamations of delight from hundreds who had assembled on the decks of the steamers *Halsey* and *Holmes*, the wharf of the Ark and many smaller craft on every hand." After a short stop at the Penn Yan end of the lake, the *Mary Bell* headed back south for a special luncheon at the Grove Springs Hotel.

It made its first regular run between Hammondsport and Penn Yan on July 11 and quickly became the favorite boat on the lake. Between the

The *Mary Bell* is seen here all decked out in banners leaving Hammondsport.

summer of 1892 and just before the U.S. entrance into World War I, the *Mary Bell* made regularly scheduled runs, was used for moonlight cruises during the summer and made special excursions for church and school groups, veterans' organizations, family reunions, etc.

The *Mary Bell* had a few flaws. Its six-foot draught meant that the captain had to be careful not to run aground going into some docks, and there were times when low water meant that it couldn't go into the outlet to the steamboat landing in Penn Yan. Its capacity was listed at 650 passengers, but there were times when it took on as many as 1,000. Sitting lower in the water, waves would occasionally wash over its gunwales in rough water. Such an occasion occurred in 1893, when Captain Harry Morse had the *Mary Bell* off the end of Bluff Point and a sudden thunderstorm blew down the lake. As the storm increased in intensity, some of the more timid on board became frightened. One of the passengers was a poet from Mississippi named Booth Lowrey, who was in the area to speak at a chautauqua at Keuka College. He overheard someone say, "Don't worry, Harry's at the wheel." Well, the storm blew over and the *Mary Bell* made its way to Penn Yan. By the time it got there, Lowrey had written this poem titled "Harry's at the Wheel":

The crowds were surging fore and aft
The waves were rolling high,
The blackened clouds are marching forth,
And war is in the sky;
The Storm King hurls his sheeted bolts
Above and all around
And hill and valley echo back
The awe-inspiring sound.
But clouds may burst and winds may roar
And vessels rock and reel,
In triumph we will plow the waves,
For Harry's at the wheel.

See how the trees along the shore
Are bending humbly down;
See how the quivering meadows writhe
Beneath the storm cloud's frown;
See how the armored whitecaps rise
Like warships off the shore,
Then dash in fury each on each
And sink to rise no more.
Our gallant vessel quivers now
From topmost deck to keel,
But we'll defy the fiercest storm
While Harry's at the wheel.

Then frown, O Storm King, in your wrath
And hurl your bolts of fire;
Bring all your shadowed legions forth
To join a conflict dire.
The heaving bosom of the lake
In frenzy writhes beneath
And fiery daggers gleam above
From many a blackened sheath.
But we'll defy your howling blast
And furious thunder peal,
For we're aboard the **Mary Bell**
And Harry's at the wheel.

The *Penn Yan*, circa 1915, is shown at the dock at Central Point. The upper deck was removed, which lowered the pilothouse.

The Erie Railroad renamed the *Mary Bell* in 1905, and it became the *Penn Yan*. For the next ten years, it operated as it had in the past. However, one of the complaints about the Erie's ownership of the Lake Keuka Navigation Company was that it neglected maintenance of the boats. That became apparent with the *Penn Yan* in the 1907 season. On one occasion, one of the propeller shafts broke, and the boat had to dock at O-go-ya-go along the shore of Bluff Point. The crew had to unload all the freight and the fifty passengers and then work the pumps to keep the boat afloat. The passengers, terribly inconvenienced, had to wait for other boats to take them to their destinations. Not long after that, while heading up the east branch toward Penn Yan with 150 passengers, many of whom planned to connect with the train, the main flue blew out, and steam from the boiler started to escape into the boat. The crew aimed streams of water into the engine room to quench the fire in the boiler, and that led to fear among the passengers that the boat was on fire. The passengers, meanwhile, were put on the shore and forced to wait for other boats to come by and take them to their destinations. The flue had blown out on at least one earlier occasion. The boat was near Urbana heading toward Hammondsport. The fireman, Fred Maxfield of Penn Yan, was in the pit when it happened. "From the pit

Penn Yan 1907

The *Penn Yan*, formerly the *Mary Bell*, docked at Gibson Landing with White Top Winery in the background. The Erie Railroad added the stripes to its stack along with the "E" in the diamond logo.

below the decks came an awful din of the roar of escaping steam and as soon as possible the engines were brought to a standstill. The boat crew was then horrified to see running up the ladder leading to the pit a figure wrapped in flames. The person hastened to the side of the boat and dropped to the water below. He was so exhausted that he was with difficulty rescued."[15] The local newspapers feared that he was burned severely enough that he would die, although he lived for another forty-one years. The *Chronicle* later reported, "The *Penn Yan* is one of the handsomest boats on any inland lake but should be made secure against these frequent mishaps."[16]

The increased use of automobiles and gas-powered pleasure boats led to a further decline in steamboat traffic. After years of heavy use, the *Penn Yan* looked old, and that led local people to question its seaworthiness. In 1915, the Erie Railroad decided to upgrade the old boat. It took out the steam boilers and installed gasoline-powered engines. It removed the top deck and rebuilt the pilothouse on the second deck. It claimed that the boat would draw ten inches less water, but top speed would only be fifteen miles per hour. The boat never ran the same. Vibrations from the new gasoline engines were uncomfortable to passengers and loosened rivets in the steel hull. Business on the *Penn Yan* dropped off further, and it was used mainly for freight and eventually tied up at the dock at Hammondsport in 1918, where it sat idle for nearly four years.

In the summer of 1922, the *Penn Yan* was put back in service for excursions. It was leased from the Erie Railroad by a firm from Rochester, the Lake Keuka Marketing Company. It was used in August for a few moonlight excursions. With an orchestra on board and dancing, it was scheduled to make three trips a week. By mid-September, it was reported in the *Yates County Chronicle* that "the attempt to revive the passenger traffic on the lake has not proven to be much of a success." In a retrospective in the *Chronicle Express* on March 27, 1941, titled "Ten Years Ago," it was written:

> *She was tied up at the dock at Hammondsport where the elements rapidly caused the once majestic queen of the Lake Keuka waves to succumb to ignominy and decadence, A few weeks ago (March of 1931) it was found that her hull had started to rot and the demolishing of the boat was begun. The brass and iron which had added to her regal appearance 40 years ago, was junked and the hulk of the old steamer is being carried away to save her from sinking in the small harbor at Hammondsport.*

CRICKET (1894–1909)

Charles Drake enjoyed the monopoly of steamboat service held by the LKNC. He owned the Bath & Hammondsport Railroad, the largest resort on the lake (the Grove Springs Hotel), major docking facilities and six large steamboats. After 1892, rates increased for both freight and passengers (from ten to twenty-five cents), as there was no competition.

That situation changed abruptly in the fall of 1894. Among Penn Yan businessmen, basket makers and farmers on the north end of Keuka Lake, there was concern about the increased fares and the fact that Drake's company favored his railroad in Hammondsport. The fear was that Hammondsport would grow as a commercial center at the expense of Penn Yan. Onto the scene came Penn Yan grocer (and grape shipper) Sam McMath. McMath was the head of the Businessman's Association and started to raise finances to build a new boat. He put a large amount of his own money into it, as did Philo Lee of Bluff Point. Shares were sold at $100 each to reach the goal. Alonzo Springstead of Geneva was contracted to do the construction (his eighth and final Keuka steamer).

The *Cricket* was the last steamboat built on Keuka Lake and the last boat built by Alonzo Springstead.

Construction started on the *Cricket* near the Ark at the Penn Yan end of the lake in early July 1894 and was completed by September 1, at which time a launching ceremony was held. There had been some talk of naming the new boat the "Samuel McMath," but McMath himself decided to name it *Cricket*, which was what he called his eldest daughter, Chrissy. It was Chrissy who broke a large bottle of champagne on the bow of her namesake as it gracefully slid into the waters of Keuka Lake.

The new steamer was grandly decorated, and Old Glory floated proudly at her stern. On board at the time of the launch were a number of those personally interested, together with invited friends of both sexes. Everything being in readiness, Mr. Samuel McMath standing at the bow made a few remarks saying, among other things, that this boat was constructed by some of the people for the use of the people and should any opposition be manifested by enemies, those enemies would be promptly killed—by kindness. He added "She is small, but we call her Cricket." As these words were uttered, the Cricket *glided out into the channel amid cheers from the crowd on the shore while the* Mary Bell, *which had just left the dock at Penn Yan and was coming around the bend, blew her whistle as a salute.*[17]

Left: Philo Lee, one of the owners of the *Cricket*, was its first captain.

Below: The *Cricket* is seen here on an excursion in Brandy Bay. Keuka College's Ball Hall is in the right background.

In less than three weeks, the engines and boiler were fitted, trial runs were made and *Cricket* was ready for business. It was ninety feet long, eighteen feet at the beam, with twin propellers and could carry as many as 350 passengers. *Cricket* was the last steamboat built on Keuka Lake and the last one built by Alonzo Springstead before he moved to Florida. Philo Lee was the owner

Sam McMath was the "Grape King" and one of the *Cricket*'s owners. The boat was named after his daughter Chrissy.

(the Lee Line) and its first captain, and Howard Stone was the pilot. The company announced it would charge ten cents to passengers one way to any place on the lake.

Cricket's owners knew that challenging the monopoly, the LKNC, would have its difficulties, and it did. The major issue was docking rights. *Cricket*'s owners had built docks in the Penn Yan outlet and in the basin at Branchport, but LKNC used its influence to prevent *Cricket* from docking in Hammondsport or any of the major resorts such as the Keuka Hotel or the Grove Springs Hotel. LKNC bought up docks at stops the *Cricket* wanted to use, and the *Cricket*'s owners would then build docks nearby. There was even a major lawsuit over the use of the dock at the Grove Springs Hotel that bounced around in the courts for years. LKNC also had a practice of luring away crew members of the *Cricket* with higher wages. There was an ugly incident in 1896, when the LKNC put the *Urbana* on the Penn Yan–Branchport run, mainly to challenge *Cricket* for business. At some point, there was a minor collision between the two boats. *Urbana*'s pilot, Frank Conklin, was arrested, and the case went into court, where the pilot of each boat blamed the other. All in all, it was a nasty relationship until Drake sold his company to the Erie Railroad in 1904. The railroad was more interested in the freight business and less interested in the passenger trade. That cleared the way for *Cricket* to focus on excursions and special events around the lake in the summers and still handle the freight business in the fall.

In 1897, the Penn Yan, Keuka Park and Branchport Electric Railroad was built connecting those three villages. Since the *Cricket* also operated mainly between Branchport and Penn Yan, the trolley line took some business away from the boat. In 1904, the boat was bought by Samuel McMath Jr., who

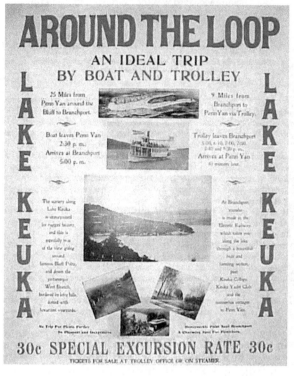

AROUND THE LOOP

AN IDEAL TRIP
BY BOAT AND TROLLEY

L A K E   K E U K A

L A K E   K E U K A

25 Miles from
Penn Yan around the
Bluff to Branchport.

Boat leaves Penn Yan
2:30 p. m.
Arrives at Branchport
5:00 p. m.

9 Miles from
Branchport to
Penn Yan via Trolley.

Trolley leaves Branchport
3:10, 4:10, 7:10, 7:50
8:40 and 9:20 p. m.
Arrives at Penn Yan
60 minutes later.

30c SPECIAL EXCURSION RATE 30c

TICKETS FOR SALE AT TROLLEY OFFICE OR ON STEAMER

"Around the Loop" was an excursion package designed to increase traffic on both the *Cricket* and the Penn Yan, Keuka Park and Branchport electric trolley.

lived in Branchport. He thought of a way to work with the trolley line to an extent. After some major upgrades to *Cricket*, an arrangement known as "Around the Loop" began in the late summer of 1905. For thirty cents, people could board the boat in Penn Yan at 2:30 p.m. and steam the twenty-five miles down the east branch of the lake into the west branch to Branchport. *Cricket* docked there around 5:00 p.m., and passengers would walk a short distance from the dock into town and catch a trolley back to Penn Yan. People had been doing that anyway, but promoting it with a special price increased its popularity dramatically. Since the last trolley left for Penn Yan at 9:30 p.m., people had plenty of time to picnic, get a meal at the hotel, catch a concert at the bandstand or do some shopping. On summer nights, it was a very pleasant forty-minute ride across the countryside back to Penn Yan.

In spite of the Lee Line's cooperation with the trolley, the electric road continued to take business away from *Cricket*. Because it was becoming unprofitable, Sam McMath Jr. sold the boat in 1907 to two experienced steamboat men from Hammondsport, Alvin Stone and John Cornell, who formed the Keuka Lake Transit Company. Under the new owners, *Cricket* continued to do a successful business by filling in gaps of the schedules of the boats belonging to the Erie Railroad. The increasing unpopularity of the Erie Railroad among people around the lake worked to *Cricket*'s favor. The Erie started all its boats from the dock at Hammondsport, so *Cricket* started its day in Penn Yan. "That

The *Cricket*, at the Penn Yan dock, rolled over and sank one time when grapes were improperly unloaded. It was fairly quickly pumped out and put back in service.

the efforts of J.E. Cornell, owner of the craft, are appreciated by lake residents is attested in the fact that residents of Keuka have voted to expend about $400 in dock repairs to accommodate the *Cricket*, which is not allowed to land at the Navigation Company's dock. The steamer carries American Express and is doing a nice freight and express transportation business."[18]

Cricket sank twice in its career, once in 1902 in fourteen feet of water at the dock in Branchport when muskrats chewed a hole in the bottom of the boat. It was quickly repaired and put back in service. The second time was in November 1907. The boat was at the steamboat dock in the Penn Yan outlet unloading thirteen thousand baskets of grapes to be transferred into rail cars. After about five hundred baskets had been unloaded, the remaining load shifted, and the boat listed and began to take on water. *Cricket* was pumped out by Penn Yan firemen and again quickly returned to service. Its demise came late one January night in 1909. *Cricket* had been drawn out of the water for repairs a mile north of Hammondsport. A fire of unknown origin broke out on board. An alarm was turned in, but the Hammondsport Fire Department, because of the distance from the village, could not respond fast enough to save the boat. *Cricket* served the farmers and people of this area for almost fifteen years.

Chapter 5

A VIRTUAL EXCURSION ON THE LAKE, CIRCA 1900

The "season" for steamboats generally ended in mid-December and started up again in early April. The boats were tied up either in the Penn Yan outlet or along the dock at Hammondsport during the dead of winter. By April, the ice was off the southern and western branches of the lake. If the ice lingered on the Penn Yan end of the east branch, the boats would leave people off at Keuka College. After 1897, they could then take the trolley into Penn Yan or they would be dropped off at the Ark, which was within walking distance of the village.

The peak of the season ran from mid-May until mid-September, when local people and community organizations would just ride the boats for the day or be dropped off at a landing somewhere along the lake to picnic, swim or fish. Railroad connections brought in people from all over the Northeast to one of the resorts operating along the lakeshore. The Bath & Hammondsport Railroad brought people to Hammondsport via the Erie system. The Northern Central Railroad brought people into Penn Yan via the Pennsylvania Railroad system, and the Fall Brook Railroad brought people there on the New York Central. The steamers arranged their schedules to meet the trains and take passengers to where they wanted to go on the lake.

Visitors to the lake during the summer and early autumn who wrote about their memories and impressions usually remarked on the scenic beauty of the hillsides around Keuka—the vineyards, the farm fields and the wooded areas. The shoreline itself was largely undeveloped by today's standards. Those farm fields, woods and vineyards often came right down

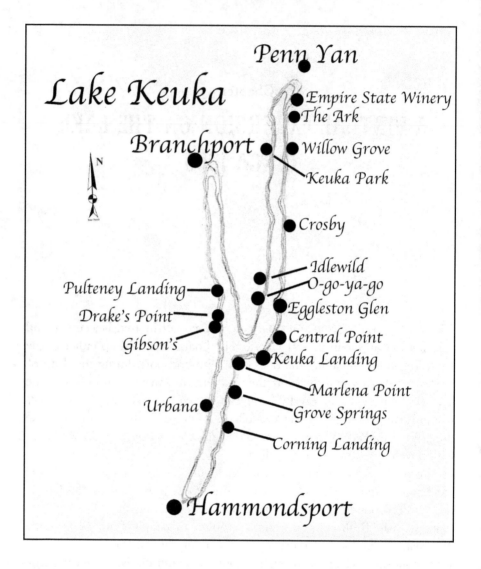

to the water's edge. Private cottages, mostly built by wealthy businessmen, began to increase in the last few decades of the nineteenth century. Many of them had their own large docks, as they were only accessible by steamboat. Also along the lake were barns, packinghouses for grapes and other types of storage facilities, especially near the small communities along the shoreline.

In order to get an idea of what it was like to go on an excursion on Lake Keuka at the peak of the steamboat era, let's theoretically board one of the boats in Penn Yan (shall we pick the *Mary Bell?*) around the turn of the twentieth century and go out on the lake. We'll do something that was rarely, if ever, done: have an excursion on all three branches. As mentioned earlier, the "main line" for the bigger steamers was a direct route from Penn Yan to Hammondsport, covering the eastern and southern branches. The west branch was less traveled, but in order to "see" where the major landings were located, we'll do all three branches. Along the way, we will pass all sixty miles of Keuka's shoreline.

PENN YAN

Penn Yan was the largest of the three villages that anchored the three branches of the lake. It had the largest and most diverse business district and served as the seat of Yates County. Penn Yan was also served by two major railroads. The Northern Central, with its depot on Jacob Street, connected to the Pennsylvania Railroad system. The Fall Brook Railroad, with its depot along the outlet, connected to the New York Central system. Between the Crooked Lake Canal in the early days, the two railroads and the steamboats, the village was a busy transportation center. Most of the activity was located around the outlet. It was originally thought that the business district of the village would be on the north end, where the roads from Canandaigua and Geneva came into Penn Yan. However, the Crooked Lake Canal, the mills along the outlet and the steamboat traffic determined that the business district would instead develop around the outlet. With workers from the canal, the steamers and later the railroads, the village developed a bit of a rowdy reputation, with plenty of taverns (thirty-two in 1885, one for every 140 inhabitants)[19] and a few "disreputable houses." The commerce pumped a lot of money into the economy, which created a vital business district and also created a wealthy class of businessmen. There were concerts, plays and lectures at the Cornwell Opera House on Main Street and later the Sampson Theater on Jacob Street. The Yates County Fairgrounds was the scene of circuses, Wild West shows and horse racing. All of that meant good business for the steamboats.

Excursionists came to Penn Yan on one of the railroads and perhaps spent a few days in one of the hotels in the village. There were several smaller hotels in Penn Yan, but the largest and most popular were the Knapp Hotel, the Central House, the Shearman House and the Benham Hotel located in the business district. If visitors chose to go on an outing on the lake, they would catch one of the horse-drawn buses or walk to the steamboat landing along the outlet.

This wagon carried passengers' trunks between the Knapp House in Penn Yan and the railroads or steamers. The passengers walked or took a hack the few short blocks.

The New York Central Railroad tracks in Penn Yan were alongside the docks so passengers had only to step off one and onto the other. The fruit house in the background still exists, although the tracks are gone.

The docks and activity related to the boats and the railroad were all just to the west of the iron bridge on Liberty Street. The original docks for the steamers were on the north side of the outlet at the foot of Pine Street (today Keuka Street). Competition between companies led to the building of docks on the south side of the outlet along Fall Brook Street (today Delano Place). The railroad being on that side guaranteed that would be the side with the greatest activity. The passengers boarded and disembarked the steamers there and the freight was unloaded, warehoused and eventually transferred to the railroad. William Wise's fruit house was there, along with Yates Lumber, Guile & Windnagle's basket factory and W.S. Harris grape juice plant.

That's also where the steamers turned around. If the boats were small enough, such as *Lulu* and *Cricket*, the deckhands simply snubbed the bow of the boat at the dock and let the current of the outlet turn it about. The larger boats, such as *Mary Bell* or *Halsey*, had to pull into Sucker Brook (which had been widened just for that purpose) and back out into the outlet to either back up to the landing or head to the lake.

People boarded the boats at the main steamboat landing (which is today part of Carey's Lumber) and went out to the lake through the channel in the outlet,

The William Wise fruit house in the left center is surrounded by boathouses on both sides of the Penn Yan harbor.

This photo illustrates how the boats turned around in Penn Yan harbor. The small boats would tie up and the current would turn them, but the larger boats had to turn in to Sucker Brook and back over to the dock.

a distance of a little over half a mile. The street on the north side of the outlet across from the main dock was called Boathouse Lane for good reason. (Today, it is Water Street connecting Liberty Street with Keuka Street.) There were over one hundred private boathouses along that side of the outlet with steam launches or fishing boats in them. The boathouses were built immediately adjacent to one another, which meant if there were a fire, it would wipe out several of them. The night the steamer *Yates* burned at the dock in 1883, three boathouses and their contents were destroyed before the blaze was put out. In 1910, a fire broke out in one, and over a dozen were destroyed.

In those days, the outlet was wider and deeper to accommodate the large boats. Lake level was kept as high as possible in order to maintain that depth. In periods of drought when the water level dropped, the boats let their passengers off at a dock at the entrance to the outlet or at the Ark a mile up the lake. A sandbar had a tendency to build up where the creek from Kimball's gully emptied into the outlet, and at least one boat, the steam barge *Springstead*, got hung up on it. Another problem was sediment seeping into the channel from the swamp to the west in front of the cemetery. In the 1890s, a long wooden dike was installed to prevent that. The state dredged the channel in 1887 and not again for many years. In 1913, William Wise (the grape dealer) and several other Penn Yan businessmen went to Albany to lobby legislators to have it dredged again.

The *Mary Bell*, in the outlet at Penn Yan, is steaming out into the lake. A fence was later built to prevent grass from the marsh (on the left) from fowling the props and paddle wheels of the boats. Pilings from that fence can still be seen.

The outlet and the north end of the east branch were always the first to freeze over in the winter. During those times, the boats from Hammondsport would dock at Keuka College, and (after 1897) the passengers could take the trolley into downtown Penn Yan. The pilots on the boats had to be especially careful coming off the lake in the dark. They were able to find the entrance to the outlet by steering toward the town clock, which was on the steeple of the Presbyterian church. Once in the channel, they had to be very familiar with the turns and conditions. In November 1902, the *Holmes* was grounded entering the channel, and local papers complained that it wouldn't have happened if there were a lighthouse at the entrance. Thanks to a state legislator from Dundee, L.D. West, the state appropriated the funds to build a lighthouse. Unfortunately, it was actually constructed on Cayuga Lake because of confusion over the name of the lake. A lighthouse for Lake Keuka was finally approved by the state in 1907, but it didn't become operational until 1910. The village of Penn Yan refused to pay for the electricity since it was outside village limits, and it took that long before the state agreed to pay for it.

At the entrance to the channel was the large icehouse of Wade Shannon's Keuka Lake Ice Company. The Fall Brook Railroad tracks ended there as well. Heading south into the open waters of the lake, the first scheduled stop was at the Ark, about a mile down the east side.

THE ARK

In the summer of 1888, a man who identified himself only as "An Old Cornellian" traveled to the Finger Lakes and wrote of his experiences in *Frank Leslie's Popular Monthly* publication. He described his experiences coming to Lake Keuka:

> *Arriving via the amazingly tortuous railroad from Dresden, upon which a train of cars is never once during the whole trip in a straight line, one naturally feels "turned around" at Penn Yan. A good many inquiries are necessary in order to find the lake, of which there is no visible sign about the town save the outlet. I first followed the crowd of excursionists—tan-faced country boys and girls in picnic attire and squads of firemen and militia in imposing but uncomfortable uniforms. They were going up the lake on the* Holmes, *but as the* Holmes *lay in the outlet near the railway station, I could see that she was a moderate-sized steamboat with an immoderate crowd already on board, leaving no room for the traditional "one more."*

The Fall Brook line of the New York Central Railroad replaced the Crooked Lake Canal in the Keuka Lake outlet. Today, the track bed is the Outlet Trail.

I therefore resumed my explorations afoot in search of Crooked Lake. In response to inquiries, I received hints concerning a certain mysterious "Ark," which seemed to be a popular institution of Penn Yan, and after walking some distance beyond the outskirts of the town, I suddenly came upon it—and the lake. The "Ark" is a roomy wooden structure, making no pretensions as to architecture, but unlimited in its resources for entertainment and comfort, built on piles over the clear, transparent water. It is a delicious nook, shaded by elms, pines, and willows. Within the Ark are creature comforts enough for a second Noah with all his family and menagerie. A mineral spring bubbles up beside the roadway. Painted skiffs dance at their moorings, and the pure waters invite a plunge. Rustic tables and benches

The Ark was Keuka's first resort and a scheduled stop for all the steamboats.

*under the trees are occupied by groups who are indisputably enjoying
themselves. It seems a place of perpetual picnic. The lake at this end is only
about a mile wide, and the opposite shore outspreads a noble panorama with
its broad yellow fields, orchards, vineyards, farms and villages stretching far
to southward and shutting off the view toward Bluff Point. The charms of
Crooked Lake and the Ark lured me from the original comprehensive plan of
my lacustrine pilgrimage. I even had a rash thought of letting all the other
places go, and staying here, a Keuka lotus-eater, during the remaining days
of my vacation.[20]*

The Ark was the oldest of the Keuka resorts. After the first steamer on
the lake (the *Keuka*) was damaged beyond repair near Hammondsport, it was
brought up to the Penn Yan end of the lake, and the engine and boiler were
scrapped by the owner. A Penn Yan man named Calvin Carpenter bought
the remains of the boat for twenty-five dollars in 1849. He kept the cabins
intact and loaded them onto a scow. When his wife first saw it, she said that
it looked like Noah's ark—and the name stuck. Carpenter tied it up at a few
different locations, but in 1850, he decided to moor it near a sulphur spring
on land that he eventually bought along the east side of the lake in Milo, less
than a mile from Penn Yan (currently 133 East Lake Road).

Calvin Carpenter owned the Ark for thirty years and turned it into an
institution at "the foot of the lake." In 1873, he demolished the original
floating Ark and built a much more substantial building that partially
extended out over the water.

*It was one of the show spots of this section, and every visitor to Penn Yan
was taken "up to the Ark" as a matter of regular, routine entertainment.
Very few strangers got out of town without having paid a visit to the Ark.
Nor was it because of the romance which surrounded the landing of the
Ark, nor the quaint ingenuity of its landlord which gave the place a special
interest. It was the sulphur springs which first gave it fame and which have
preserved its ascendancy until the present time. To go to the Ark for a jug of
water has been a common thing for many of our citizens for many years.[21]*

An Adirondack-style gazebo with seating was built over the sulphur spring,
but that was just one attraction at the resort. With five acres and nearly 1,500
feet of shoreline, there were hiking paths and picnic areas. Mr. and Mrs.
Carpenter offered meals and concessions, which included ginger ale and ice
cream. There was swimming in the lake, sulphur baths and rowboats to rent.

The Gazebo at the Ark housed the spring. The supposed healthy effect of the sulphur water was the reason for the Ark's existence.

On weekends and holidays like the Fourth of July, there were concerts by one of the bands or orchestras in Penn Yan and plenty of room for dancing. Children were intrigued by Mr. Carpenter's cage of white mice and Mrs. Carpenter's talkative parrots. One of Mrs. Carpenter's parrots, Polly, even rated a regular obituary in the *Yates County Chronicle* when it died in 1878. It was described as being "not less than forty-two years of age" and "a very intelligent and talkative bird" with a larger than average vocabulary.[22]

There were also rooms available at the Ark accommodating as many as fifty people. The Keuka Yacht Club held many of its regattas there beginning in 1872. In 1880, when the Carpenters became too old to run the place, it was sold to David E. Dewey from Canandaigua. Mr. and Mrs. Dewey ran it for fourteen years and built on the reputation achieved by Calvin Carpenter. He put a merry-go-round on the property, and his lemon beer became a popular summertime treat.

The Ark was one of the easiest resorts on Keuka to reach, being the first scheduled steamboat stop out of Penn Yan. There were a few steam launches that acted as water taxis in between scheduled leaving times for the larger boats. Being only a mile down the lake, it was easy to row to the Ark from the outlet. Mr. Dewey even operated a horse-drawn bus to meet people getting off the trains in Penn Yan, with another stop at the four corners in the business section.

> *"Al-l-l A-a-aboard! Last Ark bus tonight!" So Ed Dewey used to announce on a summer night to all pleasure-minded people in Penn Yan in the late 1880s. And usually his long-drawn announcement would attract a bus full. Then with a roaring laugh, as he cracked some quip with a passenger or by-stander, he would climb into the driver's seat and roll away over the streets, the rattling bridge, and the East Lake Road to the Ark, where some of Dewey's famous lemon beer would quickly wash down the dust inhaled on the fast mile trip.*[23]

In the 1890s, when the bicycling craze hit the area, a cinder path was put in between the Yates County Fairgrounds on Lake Street in Penn Yan and the Ark. Being less than a mile from the village limits, it was an easy walk for many people.

David Dewey died in 1894, and his widow leased the Ark out for a while. She eventually sold it in 1903 to her brother, Fred Swarts. Swarts had run the Shearman House on Elm Street in Penn Yan since 1888 and had leased the Ark for a few years in the late 1890s. He built a one-hundred-foot pier out into the lake so the steamers could dock even in times of low water. Within a year of taking possession of the resort, he decided to tear down the main building and use the lumber to build several cottages on that location. The land around the sulphur spring was eventually sold in 1910 to Penn Yan businessman Clinton Struble, who sponsored a contest in the local newspapers to rename the property. The winning entry submitted by a Penn Yan woman was Bimini Springs. She claimed that the meaning of the word "bimini" is "persons partaking of the water will be cured." The new name never took with the public, and it continued to be widely known as the Ark. Struble leased the land to several individuals who had big plans to restore the resort to its former prominence, but that didn't happen. The

The Ark, seen from the south, was very popular with tourists and locals who could walk or ride their "wheels" the short distance from Penn Yan.

Ark's popularity dropped off considerably as other resorts farther down the lake began to attract large numbers of people. Also, the trolley built in 1897 from Penn Yan to Branchport diverted many people's attention to the west side of the lake. Eventually, the land that the Ark had been on was divided and sold as lots for cottages.

Opposite the Ark on the west side was the municipal water and steam generating plant, built in 1894. The Penn Yan, Keuka Park and Branchport electric trolley was completed in 1897. That led to farmers on the west side selling off lots between the track and the lake. The result was a rash of cottage building in the late 1890s and early 1900s. The trolley line also built an icehouse just south of the water plant and harvested ice in late winters.

Willow Grove

After the Ark, the next scheduled stop was at Willow Grove, about three miles down the lake on the east side. This was one of the earliest summer settlements on Keuka. The land was once part of a farm owned by the

The *Yates* stopped at Willow Grove, a popular flag stop during the summer months.

Thayer family. Archie Thayer was a popular steamer captain on the lake following the Civil War. For twenty years, he served on the *Steuben*, *Yates*, *Lulu* and *Urbana*. In 1887, at the age of fifty-six, he decided to leave the boats and focus on his farm in Milo. A few years later, he decided to subdivide the part of his land that formed a point out into the lake and sell off twenty-two lots. There was a narrow dirt road that connected this point to Penn Yan, so with that accessibility, the lots sold off rather quickly. Summer cottages were built with names like Happy Thought, Fairview, Dew Drop In and Hopewell. The many willow trees on the point gave the community its name. What had earlier been just a flag stop dock for area farmers became a very busy seasonal stop.

KEUKA PARK

The next stop was directly across the lake from Willow Grove at the dock for Keuka Park. The small community there received a major boost around 1890 when the Free Will Baptists bought up the Ketchum farm and made plans to build a college. It was a ride on a Keuka steamer that made them decide on the location. They had been looking at a site near Seneca Lake in Eddytown (today Lakemont), where Starkey Seminary was located. However, Penn Yan had a core of aggressive, forward-looking businessmen at that time who were committed to the future financial growth of the community. They were heavily invested in the steamboat lines, they were building a new state-of-the-art opera house on Main Street and some of them wanted Penn Yan to be a college town. They invited the Baptist search committee to come to Penn Yan, took them out on Keuka Lake on a steamer to impress them with the scenery and then took them to the Gibson House off the end of the bluff for dinner. On the way back to Penn Yan, they cruised slowly past Ketchum's point. This was farmland that wasn't doing well; the soil had too much clay to be successful. The committee thought this location was ideal—fairly level and far enough removed from the distractions of Penn Yan. Communities around the lake raised $50,000 in pledges to begin the project of bringing the school here. The driving force behind getting the school started was Dr. George H. Ball of Buffalo, one of the members of that original Baptist committee. Ground was broken for the main building in 1888, and for many years, it was the only building on the campus. The bricks were made from that same clay that made the point a poor spot for farming. Thirty years later, the building was officially named Ball Hall.

The *Halsey* is seen here passing Keuka College. The reliable steamboat service was part of the reason for the college being located near Penn Yan.

Electric Park was a recreation area on the electric trolley line midway between Penn Yan and Branchport. This was where its DC electric generating plant was located.

The college was a major business boost for the steamboats when it opened in 1890. It meant transporting students and their families to and from Keuka Park. The college also sponsored events that appealed to the general public. The assemblies and chautauquas held there each summer, as well as the dramatic productions, lectures and concerts, brought large numbers of people to Keuka Park and kept the boats busy.

In 1897, when the Penn Yan, Keuka Park and Branchport electric railway was completed, the trolley company placed its power station just to the north of the college along Brandy Bay. On land it owned but didn't use, it created a park called Electric Park. The park became quite popular as a picnic grounds for local people and organizations. A dance pavilion was built, and the trolley and the boats brought people in for dancing and concerts.

CROSBY

Continuing southward along the eastern shore, the boat would pass several landings that were flag stops for farmers or private cottages, the most notable of which was Finton's Landing on the east side. That was a busy stop during the grape harvest, as there was a basket factory and packinghouse there. A little farther down on the east side, about seven miles outside Penn Yan, are two points that extend well out into the lake. Between these two points was the small community of Crosby. Joseph Crosby had a farm there and was the first to grow grapes on that part of the lake. He was a county sheriff in the 1860s and owned one of the steamboat companies in the 1870s. His company owned the *George R. Youngs* steamer and had the *Yates* built. It was involved in the steamboat wars of the 1870s and eventually sold out. Crosby, the settlement, had a basket-making factory, store, post office, school and church. The landing there served not only that community but also the farmers in the town of Barrington.

IDLEWILD

Idlewild is one of the most beautiful and attractive landings on Lake Keuka. It is on the Bluff Point side of the East Branch, and in days of popular navigation, many excursionists and summer sojourners passed very pleasant vacation periods in and about the shady grounds and in the neat and well-kept house of public accommodation by the genial Pascal T. VanLiew. He kept a trim and speedy pleasure boat named "Minnie V." for trips on the lake. Idlewild was a favorite resort of people from all sections.[24]

Crossing the lake to the east side of Bluff Point and continuing south, the boat would pass several more flag stops on Bluff Point that served private cottages owned by wealthy Penn Yan and Rochester businessmen. The cottages had names like the Parsonage, Kill Kare, Maple Point, Sycamore Point and Heart's Content. There was also a major farm dock, Dunning's, that in the summer months served as a drop-off spot for swimmers, picnickers and fishermen.

In a heavily wooded area along the shoreline were two popular hotels, the first of which was the Idlewild Hotel, which opened for business on the Fourth of July 1879. It was run by Pascal VanLiew, who had earlier run a hotel in Dresden on Seneca Lake and also had worked for a while on the Keuka steamboats. Like O-go-ya-go, which was a short distance to the south, Idlewild was only accessible by boat, and the two hotels were close enough that they shared a dock. VanLiew had a fleet of twenty-one rowboats for guests to use, so the hotel was popular with fishermen. He also had Alonzo Springstead build him a steam yacht, the *Minnie V.*, which was used to take guests out onto the lake. The Idlewild Hotel was popular with young people in the area, as there was a large dancing pavilion with bands hired on weekends.

Over the years, Idlewild developed a somewhat dodgy reputation. After the town of Jerusalem went "dry" in 1898, it was known to sell alcohol illegally and was the scene of several fistfights.

> *In those days the Sunday excursions came down the lake to Idlewild and Ogoyago. Along the wooded path between the two hotels were often camped men with little tables, three shells, and a little black ball. They invited the passersby to pick out the shell under which the little ball reposed and be rewarded with a five or ten dollar bill. Sometimes when business was dull, these gentlemanly sharks would play for the insignificant sum of one or two dollars. Of the many who tried to locate the ball, only the "cappers" were successful. It did not take long for twenty-five dollars to change hands on those Sunday afternoons.* [25]

"Cappers" were part of the shell game operation. They would appear to win, and that would encourage onlookers to play the game.

Sometime in the early 1900s, Idlewild ceased to operate as a hotel and became a private residence. One of the most notorious murders in the history of Yates County occurred there in 1911. Charles Sprague, who was living in the old hotel at the time with his wife and children, had a major disagreement with a neighbor over a patch of potatoes that Sprague had worked. Sprague got a gun and shot his neighbor twice, killing him. In a long, drawn-out trial, Sprague was convicted of murder, sentenced to death and sent to Auburn Prison for execution. What followed were three years of attempts to declare a mistrial and appeals. In May 1916, Charles Sprague became the last person to be executed at Auburn Prison.

> *But Idlewild today (1912) is but a shadow of its former self. No longer do the whitewashed stones along the walk glisten in the sunlight; no longer do crowds congregate under the front edge of the porch and try to swing the*

string so the ring on the end of it would catch on the nail some distance away. Idlewild, once the rendezvous of youth and beauty, where the harp and the violin have furnished inspiration for the swaying waltz and the sedate lancers, is now known best as the scene of an awful tragedy.[26]

O-GO-YA-GO

A more quiet, shady and delightful spot than O-go-ya-go is hard to be found on Lake Keuka. The grounds are well kept and little or no sun is experienced throughout the day. The hotel is neat and comfortable and especially well kept by Mr. Andrew Jobbitt. At present the house is comfortably well filled

O-go-ya-go was a resort on the bluff. The only access to it was by steamboat.

with season guests and large numbers of daily visitors are entertained. One hundred and seventy-five transients took dinner there last Thursday. Parties desiring rest and quiet for a day or season should visit O-go-ya-go.[27]

Just a short distance to the south of the Idlewild Hotel was the resort called O-go-ya-go. The name came from the Seneca tribe of the Iroquois, and it is said that is what they first called the lake before they called it Keuka. *O-go-ya-go* is translated as either "across the water" or "between the waters," which would certainly be an appropriate description of Bluff Point. An original building burned in the early 1890s and was quickly rebuilt. The hotel had only ten rooms for boarders, which, according to the liquor laws of the time, allowed it to sell liquor on Sundays. The hotel had a dining room that could hold 175 people and a large dancing pavilion. As a result, it was a popular spot for dinner and evenings of dancing. The hotel had a beer garden and was widely known as a "booze stop" for Sunday excursionists well into the 1890s.

In 1898, the town of Jerusalem, which includes Bluff Point, voted "no license." That meant that local option prohibition closed down the bar at O-go-ya-go. Business dropped off dramatically, and the owner, facing bankruptcy, sold the land. It no longer operated as a resort. The building itself, after years as a private summer home, caught fire and was destroyed in May 1938.

EGGLESTON GLEN AND THE NATURAL SCIENCE CAMP

Returning to the eastern shore, almost directly across the lake from O-go-ya-go was the next scheduled top at Eggleston's Glen, about nine and a half

The "Rec Hall" at Camp Arey is shown here, circa 1920, when the emphasis of the camp had changed from science to sports.

miles from Penn Yan. The glen extends well up the hill to the east with a fast-moving creek and magnificent 110-foot waterfall. This was a favorite place for summertime excursionists to picnic and hike. The Keuka Hotel and the hotel at Grove Springs ran special boats for their guests to Eggleston Glen. The creek formed a large point that extends out into the lake.

In 1905, Professor Albert Arey bought the 165 acres on the point and moved his Natural Science Camp over from Canandaigua Lake. Although billed as a natural science camp, it had a military look, and the emphasis was on physical fitness and sports for boys. Reveille was at 6:30 a.m. and Taps at 9:45 p.m. The camp was self-sufficient, generating its own electricity, growing vegetables and maintaining a dairy. Eventually, the camp accepted girls as well. Most of the two hundred or so campers came from the New York City area. Courses were offered in photography, electricity and geology. It had the distinction of being the oldest and largest natural science camp in the United States.

Central Point

Continuing south along the eastern shore, approaching the end of the east branch is Central Point, so named because it is exactly 11.6 miles from both Penn Yan and Hammondsport. It was a popular resort area with several

Central Point, located on Keuka's east side halfway between Hammondsport and Penn Yan, is noted today for the Victorian cottages that are today virtually unchanged from this image.

beautiful Victorian-style cottages built mostly by Corning businessmen in the 1880s. The buildings had names reflecting the ultimate goal of relaxation. "Halcyon" comes from a Greek myth and means calm and peaceful; "Sans Souci" means without worry. The cottage "Ultimatum" has an interesting story. In the late 1880s, the Ultimatum Cigar Co. in Ithaca went bankrupt and had all its property repossessed. The company owed a large sum of money to the fellow who owned that cottage, and all it could do to repay him was to give him the sign that reads "Ultimatum."

KEUKA LANDING

On the eastern shore opposite the end of Bluff Point was a collection of cottages, warehouses and hotels known as Keuka Landing, an important stop. It was generally believed that the best fishing on Lake Keuka was off the end of Bluff Point where the three branches of the lake come together. It was only natural, then, that fishermen would be attracted to that area. Seth Green (1817–1888) did much to enhance Keuka's reputation among avid fishermen in the years following the Civil War. He reported that one day in 1880, he took with hook and line nineteen salmon trout weighing 113 pounds and, on another day, thirty-three black bass weighing 106 pounds. Green had a growing national reputation as the "Father of Fish Culture." In 1864, he built the first fish hatchery in the world at Caledonia, New York, to the west of Keuka. He stocked fish in rivers, lakes and streams all over the country. It was on Keuka that he invented the treble hook and what became known as the Seth Green rig to catch lake trout. Green claimed that Lake Keuka was "unsurpassed by any waters in America as a fishing resort." When he came to Keuka, he would often stay at a small hotel near a cluster of summer homes in what became known as Keuka village opposite the end of Bluff Point on the east branch of the lake.

That small hotel where Green stayed was eventually owned and run by James M. Washburn. In 1894, with his business booming, Washburn decided to build a larger hotel. What was known as both the Washburn Hotel and the Keuka Hotel became one of the most popular resorts on the lake. A promotional booklet published by the Lackawanna Railroad said that Washburn's hotel was an ideal retreat for the tired city worker that accommodates one hundred people at eight to twelve dollars a week: "Delightfully situated on a bluff overlooking Lake Keuka, which affords

This postcard image shows the *Penn Yan* and the *Yates* or *Steuben* docked at the Keuka Hotel. Note the smaller private steamer in the foreground.

excellent sailing, fishing and rowing; the lake is abundantly stocked with salmon, trout, black bass and other varieties of fish; house is modern and homelike in every particular; cuisine unsurpassed, table being supplied with the best of fresh fruits, vegetables, butter, eggs, etc."[28]

In 1904, James Washburn decided to sell the Keuka Hotel and move to Rochester to educate his children. It was sold to Andrew Tracy from Binghamton for $12,000. Tracy ran the hotel successfully for a number of years and then decided that he wanted to return to his farm near Binghamton. In 1912, he sold the hotel to a wealthy young widow from Philadelphia who had two small sons. Bessie Young had bought a summer cottage in Keuka village just a few years earlier and had gotten to know Tracy quite well. "Mr. Tracy kidded Mrs. Young about the numerous free meals she served. He said that she ought to buy the hotel and make them pay for their meals. Mrs. Young responded that 'You draw up an option and I will.' He walked over to his register, came back with a paper which she signed, and that was it."[29]

Although Bessie Young had no experience at all in the hotel business, she became the spirit of the Keuka Hotel. She took an already successful business and, through her innovations and promotions, made it more so.

The Keuka Hotel was centrally located on the east side of the lake. All boats on the Penn Yan to Hammondsport route stopped at Keuka.

Bessie decided at the beginning that she would keep the hotel open all year and appeal to area residents, excursionists off the steamboats, fishermen, duck hunters, etc. Her promotional booklet emphasized the fine wineries around the lake, the efficient steamboat and railroad service and the great fishing. "This is the hotel nearest the trout fishing grounds and every season the house is crowded with enthusiastic disciples of Isaac Walton. The place is home-like and the cuisine is unsurpassed. There is no quieter or better conducted place on the lake, where the formalities of fashionable life may be discarded and genuine rest and recreation found."[30]

Bessie Young immediately began to upgrade the facility. She had a seawall built to beautify the grounds and protect the building in periods of high water. There were thirty rooms for guests but originally only one bathroom, so she installed additional bathrooms. Mrs. Young enlarged the kitchen and, in November 1912, built a pavilion out over the lake to serve as a dance hall. She focused on high-quality vocalists, bands and orchestras for entertainment. The plan was to bring in young people and community organizations, as well as the regular clientele.

The dance hall at the Keuka Hotel is depicted in this postcard image. It was later turned ninety degrees and converted to a roller-skating rink, existing into the 1950s.

The Keuka Hotel far outlasted the era of the steamboats on the lake. Its best years were from the late 1920s until World War II. Mrs. Young electrified the hotel in the late 1920s and continued to keep hotel facilities up to date. In an interview at the time of her retirement in 1966, she said, "All I wanted was good music—I didn't care if they were just starting out or already known."[31] She brought in some of the great names of the big band era: Rudy Vallee, Paul Whiteman, Fred Waring and Glen Miller. The story is often told that Hoagy Carmichael wrote the lyrics to his signature hit "Stardust" on a napkin while he was a member of the house band in the late 1920s. It is a great story, but it doesn't stand up to research. Carmichael wrote the music to "Stardust" but not the lyrics, which were written a few years later by a fellow named Mitchell Parish. There is a historic marker in front of a building in downtown Bloomington, Indiana, Carmichael's hometown, that states, "Hoagy wrote that he composed Stardust in part on the piano of the Bookstore located here." It says "in part"; therefore, he could have worked on it a bit while at the Keuka Hotel. There is also a hotel on Raquette Lake in the Adirondacks that claims he wrote the music there.

The Keuka Hotel was a lively spot on the lake in the 1920s and 1930s. Franklin Delano and Eleanor Roosevelt stayed there while he was campaigning for governor in 1928. Glenn Curtiss flew in by seaplane. There were roadsters and flapper girls. At times, the hotel served booze during Prohibition and occasionally got caught with illegal slot machines. In its heyday, the Keuka Hotel was *the* place to be.

After Mrs. Young's retirement, her son Sherwood ran the hotel for a few years, but Bessie remained part of the scene. When she died in 1969, Sherwood closed the hotel. At the time, he said, "Mother was the hotel. When she died, the bottom fell right out of it."[32] The contents were auctioned off in 1973, and the building itself was sold and demolished in 1974. The five hundred feet of lake frontage was subdivided into cottage lots.

When the Keuka Hotel was built in 1894, another building on the site had to be relocated. It was bought by Frank Switzer and moved a short distance to the south and was called the Switzerland Inn. It quickly became a popular gathering place. Also at Keuka Landing was a smaller hotel called Helvetia House operated by Carl Schmoker. He was of Swiss descent, and Helvetia was the name given by the Romans to the area that

The freight dock at Keuka village was a primary shipping point for much of the produce of the east side of Keuka, except for grapes, which shipped from many farmers' docks.

includes modern Switzerland. In addition to the hotel, Schmoker also ran a boat livery. Keuka Landing was a popular area for fishermen as well as summer excursionists. In the fall, its central location on the lake made it a major shipping point for area farmers, especially for shipping grapes. There were warehouses and other storage facilities. Theodore Campbell, who served as dock agent at Keuka for the steamboat company for twenty-three years, remembered that at harvest time, there were often as many as twenty wagons lined up in order to unload at his dock. He reported that at times as many as fifty thousand baskets of grapes were loaded on the boats in a season and seventy-five thousand bushels of buckwheat.[33]

From Keuka Landing, we'll steam across the "wide waters" of the lake where the three branches meet. Up on the end of Bluff Point is a large southern-style mansion with a magnificent view looking south up the lake. Built by Abraham Wagener in 1833, it was a landmark throughout the entire steamboat era. Sturdevant's Landing, on the end of the bluff, was a key landing for the farmers of the area. We'll round the end of the bluff and head north about seven miles to the end of the west branch and the small village of Branchport. Along the eastern shoreline (Bluff Point) there were a few flag stop docks and just a few cottages. During the era of the steamboats, the west branch of the lake was the least developed of the three branches, and there were far fewer people living in Branchport than in Penn Yan or Hammondsport.

BRANCHPORT

Realizing that a railroad connection would be the key to their economic growth, businessmen in Branchport tried desperately to get one in the 1870s and 1880s, attempting to connect to the Fall Brook Railroad coming out of Penn Yan or the Bath & Hammondsport line or the Middlesex Valley Railroad out of Gorham—all to no avail. As a result, the steamboat companies did not provide Branchport with the same level of service that they did Penn Yan or Hammondsport.

Over the years, the void was filled by smaller boats. In the 1870s, the fifty-foot steam yacht *Lilly* ran a regular schedule from Branchport to Hammondsport and Penn Yan. Between 1878 and 1895, the seventy-five-foot *Lulu* was based in Branchport and ran a regular schedule. Starting in 1883, the sixty-foot *West Branch* provided regular service to Branchport in

The dock at Branchport appears to be a gathering place for youth on Sundays.

competition with *Lulu.* The community favored *Lulu* since that boat was based there, and the *West Branch* eventually serviced other parts of the lake. For a few years, between 1904 and 1907, the ninety-foot steamer *Cricket* made regular runs between Penn Yan and Branchport with the Lee Line's "Around the Loop" special. Excursionists boarded the boat in Penn Yan and went down the east branch of the lake, around Bluff Point and up the west branch to Branchport. That brought a boost to the local economy, as passengers would get off the boat at the dock in the basin, walk into the business area and shop or eat in the hotel before catching the trolley back to Penn Yan. It was a very popular excursion.

In approaching the basin where the Branchport docks were located, the boats had to enter a channel cut through the sandbar that is still there today. The channel was clearly marked during the day but apparently not at night. The October 1, 1874 issue of the *Yates County Chronicle* reported:

> *The new steamboat,* Lilly, *makes daily trips from this place to Penn Yan, stopping for passengers and freight at any point on the West Branch. The terms will be reasonable and it is to be hoped that patronage will be freely given to this new and desirable enterprise. A small pier should be built near the channel through the bar and a light be shown thereon at night for the guidance of the various lake craft. Very nearly a fatal accident occurred*

on Saturday night for want of a fixed light. Richard Craig was piloting the steamer in a small skiff with a lantern, when he was struck by the steamboat, sent sprawling into the water and not easily rescued. Luckily he escaped with only a bath and a fright.

Eventually, fixed lights marked the entrance.

Pulteney Landing

Heading south toward Hammondsport and staying along the western shore of the lake, the first major stop was Pulteney Landing about four and a half miles from Branchport. The point had several names over the years depending on who owned it. It was called Boyd's Point and Nichol's Point but was most widely known as Pulteney Landing. The village of Pulteney is just up the hill, and the residents could catch the steamers there. This was another major shipping point for grapes and other farm products.

A major temperance event was held at Pulteney Landing in July 1884. As the grape culture and the number of wineries grew around the lake, so did the temperance movement. The Woman's Christian Temperance Union (WCTU) was thriving in both Yates and Steuben Counties, as was a group called the Good Templars. In 1901, Carrie Nation was a headline speaker at the Yates County Fair. There were constant attempts, mostly successful, to vote the townships around the lake dry ("no license"). For three days in July 1884, the great Lake Keuka Temperance Camp Meeting was held at Pulteney Landing. The boat lines, in connection with the railroads, ran special excursions to the landing with the *Holmes* and *Urbana*, and on each of the three days, over one thousand people listened to speeches by some of the national leaders of the temperance movement. The camp meeting invigorated the local temperance people, and a network sprang up around the lake to keep a watchful eye on the hotels and taverns to guarantee that liquor laws around the lake were being enforced.

Drake's Point

A few miles farther down along the western shore was a well-developed point with a large boathouse and a steamboat dock. On the point were

Drake Point, the summer home of James Drake from Corning, is today the location of the Lakeside restaurant.

two large Victorian cottages built by James Drake (not to be confused with Charles Drake, who owned the steamboat line between 1892 and 1904; they were of no relation). James Drake was a very wealthy banker from Corning, and this was his family's summer getaway spot. He had what was considered to be the fastest steam launch on the lake, the *Madge*, named after one of his daughters.

GIBSON'S LANDING

Staying along the western shore of the lake for about a mile, heading south toward Hammondsport, the next major landing was Gibson's opposite the end of Bluff Point. This was another major landing for the people and farmers of the area around Pulteney.

The area that eventually became known as Gibson's Landing was a popular access point for people living on the west side of Lake Keuka even before the steamboat era began. The ferryboats that took people from one side of the lake to the other stopped there. George Gibson bought one hundred acres there around the time of the Civil War and farmed much of it. Having worked on canalboats as a young man, he also developed an interest in commerce. He built a warehouse along the shore to store farm products awaiting shipment on the steamboats. Gibson also put in vineyards and was one of the organizers of the Lake Keuka Wine Company in 1878. Gibson built a stone building on his land to house parts of the wine and champagne production.

In 1887, he built a hotel at that location and called it the Gibson House. It quickly became the most popular resort on the western shore of the lake. The hotel had three stories with large verandas and sixty-five rooms and was widely known for the peaceful, shady setting and the delicious meals that were served there. The main veranda was called the Sanctum and was lit up each evening with beautiful, colored Chinese lanterns. That plus the fancy colorful paint on the building gave the hotel a festive atmosphere.

George Gibson died in 1898, and the hotel was taken over by his son. The hotel lasted far beyond the steamboat era. There is an interesting story connected with the Gibson House. In the mid-1920s, the State of New York planned to build a paved highway extending the length of the lake between Hammondsport and Penn Yan. Governor Al Smith came out from Albany to look over the situation. He was entertained by businessmen and farmers at the Keuka Hotel over on the east side of the lake, hoping that the highway would go down their side. Business interests and farmers on the west side brought the governor to the Gibson House for an outdoor picnic. On a hot, dry summer afternoon, Pulteney farmers drove their wagons back and forth on the dirt road in front of the hotel, raising clouds of dust that somewhat affected the atmosphere of the governor's lunch. Guess which side of the lake got the paved highway? Today it's Route 54A.

Immediately to the south of the Gibson House was a winery. George Gibson was one of the original owners of the Lake Keuka Wine Company, which eventually reorganized under the name White Top Winery. Gibson oversaw the construction of the stone buildings for the winery.

Grove Springs

Again crossing the "wide waters" confluence of the three branches and crossing over to the eastern shore, it is easy to see Marlena Point, which separates the southern branch of Keuka from the east branch. In the early days of the steamers, it was known as Gleason's Point. Hiram Gleason owned it and based one of the early ferries there. When Charles Drake took over the B&H Railroad and the steamboat line in the 1890s, he bought the land and renamed it after his wife (Mary) and his daughter (Lena).

About a mile south of Marlena Point, still on the eastern shore, was Grove Springs. At that location was Care Naught, the cottage originally owned by William Halsey that was later bought by Charles Drake. Just before reaching

The Grove Springs Hotel was the largest hotel on Keuka Lake. While it did not have electric lights, it did have electric bells and hot and cold running water.

the Grove Springs Hotel was a large building that housed the Keuka Club. It was bought by a group of Elmira politicians and businessmen in 1882 and for thirty years was a rest and relaxation spot for them and their families. The club was known for its fine food and genial atmosphere and was in easy walking distance of the hotel grounds.

The Grove Springs Hotel was built in 1868 by two Hammondsport businessmen, John Davis and J.M. Crane, and opened for business the next year. It was the largest resort on Lake Keuka and, at times, the most popular. Located on the eastern shore of the lake on the southern branch, it was also near the popular fishing grounds off the end of Bluff Point. The resort was only accessible by steamboat, a thirty-minute ride from the dock at Hammondsport or a ninety-minute ride from the channel in Penn Yan. It was a popular destination for local people and organizations as the extensive grounds had picnic groves, a large dance pavilion, grassy lawns, paths for walking, gardens and a fountain, as well as facilities for large meetings. Also on the grounds were a billiard parlor, a large bathhouse and tennis and croquet courts. There were boats available for fishing and a steam launch to take excursions to the glens at Hammondsport or Eggleston Point. The railroad lines widely promoted Grove Springs, and as a result, excursionists

This drawing of the Grove Springs Hotel illustrates what a grand place it was. *The* resort on Keuka Lake, it burned in 1915, not to be rebuilt.

came from all over the country to relax and enjoy the mineral baths and fine food. It was an idyllic vacation spot.

The hotel itself was three stories with large, shaded verandas. There were one hundred rooms in the main hotel and thirty-two additional apartments available in the pavilion, cottage and bathhouse. The hotel went through an extensive remodeling in 1881 and had features not found in other lakeside resorts—indoor plumbing with many rooms being en suite, gas lighting and a system of electric bells for service. In a postcard of the time written from Grove Springs, a woman tells a friend that she took a "stand-up bath" (aka a shower).

Promotional materials highlighted the health benefits of the resort for those coming out of the large, dirty and congested cities. There was a physician in residence who supervised the therapeutic mineral baths. Grove Springs advertised "Pure air, pure, clear water, a healthful climate with no mosquitos."

An 1884 brochure, *Lakeside Life in Central New York*, described the features of the resort:

> *The roomy hotel, with its ample porches, stands well back from the lake upon a gentle rising slope, surrounded by a grove of fine forest trees. Along the waterfront is an even, gravelly beach, and a strong, capacious dock is*

projected to deep water. The extensive grounds are laid out in lawns and drives with here and there a fountain, a rustic pavilion, or a flower plot to give emphasis to the scene of sweet beauty. The illustrations printed herewith will give the reader a fair idea of the immediate surroundings of the hotel, but they can convey no hint of the cool, refreshing breeze that sweeps down across the broad surface of the lake, stirring the leafy grove into a musical murmur like the rushing of far-away waters, and sending the wavelets in rapid chase along the shore.

The Grove Springs Hotel changed ownership at least eight times during its forty-six years of existence. One of the owners was Charles W. Drake who also owned the Bath & Hammondsport Railroad and the Lake Keuka Navigation Company. Unlike the Keuka Hotel with Bessie Young, none of the owners lived at Grove Springs on a regular basis. They hired managers to run the resort or else leased it out for the season. Some of the managers were excellent. The first one was an entertainer from New York City, Colonel Stephen Moore, who did much to establish the grand reputation of Grove Springs. After the extensive and expensive ($75,000) remodeling in 1881, the Fuller brothers (Dwight and George) successfully ran the resort for several years. Other managers were not so effective, and at times Grove Springs suffered from mismanagement and was forced to close temporarily. A July 1895 issue of the *Yates County Chronicle* reported:

It's too bad that the Grove Spring House remains closed. It seems, however, to have been demonstrated that the plant is a burden to all who undertake its management. We are of the opinion that it could be successfully carried on if the rates for board were not so high. Many families from Penn Yan and vicinity would be glad to take their summer outing there. It is one of the most delightful spots on the lake.

One night in December 1915, the Grove Springs Hotel—an old wood-frame building out of reach by any fire department—caught fire. The *Yates County Chronicle* described the conflagration:

GROVE SPRINGS HOUSE BURNS WITH HEAVY LOSS—Summer Hostelry Containing 100 Rooms Is Destroyed—Grove Springs hotel, the largest building of its kind on any of the Finger Lakes, burned Friday night causing a loss said to be $50,000, with some insurance. The big building was unoccupied, the present proprietors having closed it for the

The dock at the Grove Springs Hotel is seen here from the upper deck of a steamboat.

winter leaving it in charge of a caretaker. About twenty minutes after six, a blaze was seen in the upper northeast corner of the four-story frame structure, which soon enveloped the entire upper floor and one story after another crumpled, falling into the story below. Although entirely of wood, the big building burned almost all night which communicated to the grove about and finally reached the big dancing pavilion where conventions had been held for years. The blaze was seen for miles around and at Branchport the flames looked to be soaring in the air one hundred feet, while the residents on the opposite side of the lake said it was almost as bright as day in their locality.[34]

John Bertram, the last owner of the hotel, planned to rebuild the hotel on a less elaborate scale, but those plans were changed when, during a storm in May 1916, the wind collapsed the roof of the old pavilion, killing one of Bertram's workmen and injuring the owner's wife. A month later, he abandoned the project, and he eventually sold the property off in parcels.

The Urbana winery was a tourist stop for all the excursions by steamboat. It was located almost directly across from the Grove Springs Hotel, which had its own steamboat for daily visits to the winery.

URBANA

Across the lake from Grove Springs, on the western shore, was a small community that formed around the Urbana Wine Company. Guests from the Grove Springs Hotel especially enjoyed the short boat ride over to sample its Gold Seal champagne. Around the winery were several homes, most of which were residences for the workers.

Crossing the lake again and heading south along the eastern shoreline, there were a number of private cottages owned by wealthy businessmen from Elmira and Corning. The most notable is the beautiful home and point known as the Elms,

> *owned by J. Monroe Shoemaker of Elmira, who has spared neither pains nor expense in improving his property. A large cottage nestles among the huge elms with which the point is covered, and all the conveniences of city life are here. A large reservoir located on the hillside is filled with water by a steam pump and conveyed to the house in pipes. There are two boat houses on the point, one for row boats and the other for housing the "Dilma," the largest and finest naptha launch on the lake. It will carry 20 people and is often seen on the lake.*[35]

A little farther south of there is a cluster of cottages at Corning Landing, which was a regular stop in the summer months. Farther to the south, near Tanglewood Point, was the Hammondsport Club for influential young men from that village.

Hammondsport

About four miles south of Urbana was the southern end of the lake and the village of Hammondsport. The lakefront in Hammondsport provided excellent facilities for the steamboats. Water Street ran parallel to the shoreline and provided access for foot traffic and wagons. The Bath & Hammondsport Railroad entered the village along the north side of the inlet and then curved to run between Water Street and the lake, transporting both passengers and freight. The lake was kept deep enough that the large steamers could tie up right along the lakefront. The Lake Keuka Navigation Company built a 110-foot pavilion and a wharf in 1889 for passengers. There were warehouses, a dry dock area and packinghouses for the grapes. Village streets, the railroad and the boats were just yards away from one another. In 1891, electric lights were installed along the waterfront. Between April and December, it was an active and vibrant area.

Promoted by the *Hammondsport Herald* as "a Saratoga for Elmira people," there were enough attractions in Hammondsport that it became a destination for many excursionists as well as a jumping-off spot to other places around the lake. That gave an economic boost to businessmen around the village square, as well as the steamboat companies.

There were a few excellent hotels in the village. There was the Steamboat Hotel on Lake Street and the Urbana Hotel on the village square. But the largest and most popular hotel in Hammondsport was the Fairchild House. It was perfectly located on the lakefront near the railroad depot and steamboat docks. The building was originally a box factory run by two brothers, Smith and Ed Fairchild. It was converted to a hotel around the time of the Civil War. Smith joined Company A of the 161st New York Volunteer Infantry as a second lieutenant in the autumn of 1862, leaving Ed to run the business. When Smith returned from the war, he went into the steamboat business, serving as the captain of the *Lulu* for a while.

Ed Fairchild was known as an affable, accommodating host, and the meals at his establishment were known to be the best quality. Its popularity was

The Fairchild House in Hammondsport was included in most excursions with the railroad and steamboats in its front yard.

such that people complained from time to time that they couldn't get seated. Fairchild added a dance pavilion in 1884, and the Fairchild House became a popular destination, especially for the people at the north end of the lake who wanted to spend the day on the lake, have a good meal and perhaps hike up the Hammondsport Glen.

His health failing, Ed Fairchild sold the hotel in 1897 to William Wadsworth, who had been a conductor on the Erie Railroad and was quite familiar with the place. He and his wife, Lillian, ran the place until William died in 1908, and Lillian ran it alone until 1919, when the hotel, then known as the Wadsworth Hotel, closed for good.

Another popular attraction for excursionists was the Hammondsport Glen. Just a short walk from the Fairchild House was the entrance to the glen. In the mid-1870s, bridges and footpaths were put in. J.P. Barnes started to promote it, with its beautiful waterfalls, as a tourist attraction, which put it in direct competition with Watkins Glen at the head of

Orchestrion Hall in Hammondsport was a major attraction for a few years. The grounds included a beer garden in addition to the orchestrion.

Seneca Lake. The steamboat companies advertised, "Parties of 25 and upwards can make the round trip and include the picturesque Glen at Hammondsport for $1.25 each."

Just northeast of the village center, up the terraced hill toward Pulteney, was a three-story building called Orchestrion Hall. It was constructed over the winter of 1875–76 and had a commanding view of the village and the southern end of the lake. A grand orchestrion, said to be the largest in the United States at that time, was shipped over from Germany and installed at a cost of nearly $15,000. An orchestrion operated similar to a player piano but included sounds of other instruments to sound like a band or orchestra. Rolls produced the music, which was enhanced by a series of pipes. The hall had a dance floor, and the business was operated as a German-style beer garden. With the splendid view, the music, the dancing and the beer, it became hugely popular with the public and greatly enhanced excursion traffic on both the railroad and the steamboats. After twenty years, with the instrument starting to show its age, it was sold in 1895 and moved to Cincinnati. The hall minus the orchestrion served for many years after that as a community center until it was dismantled and divided into smaller buildings.

R.R. DEPOT & STEAMBOAT LANDING, HAMMONDSPORT, N.Y.

This postcard image of the Hammondsport waterfront illustrates the proximity of the trains and docks.

After 1904, when the Erie Railroad bought the steamboat company, the docks and the railroad, tension started to develop between many of the people in the village and the Erie company. There was an ugly incident in August 1910 dealing with twenty private boathouses along the lakefront. They had been allowed there by the old steamboat company even though they were on company property. The Erie Railroad wanted them removed so it could enlarge one of its grape warehouses. It gave the owners of the boathouses notice that the boathouses had to be removed. Some complied, but most didn't. One night, just after midnight, a special train arrived at the lakefront with forty laborers and several detectives to guard the tracks. They removed the boathouses. A few weeks later, the owners sued the railroad and even hinted that they would take action to have the B&H tracks removed from the village. The incident was eventually smoothed over, but it added greatly to the general dissatisfaction that was building locally with the Erie management.

Chapter 6

ACTUAL EXCURSIONS

Over the years, Keuka Lake has inspired poets, writers, artists and just everyday people. That is as true in our own time as it was back during the peak years of the steamboat era. Many who went on the actual excursions on the steamers later wrote of their experiences in local newspapers. This section is a collection of several of those stories.

PENN YAN DEMOCRAT, 1860

THE PEOPLE'S EXCURSION—One of the pleasant and memorable episodes of the season was the "People's Excursion" on the steamer Steuben *last Wednesday. The shower of Wednesday morning deterred many from making the venture; nevertheless a "right merrie and goodlie companie" appeared at the steamboat wharf in Penn Yan a little after the appointed hour and embarked for the excursion. The gay little* Steuben *was swung loose from her moorings, the ever courteous and reliable Captain Gregg laid skillful hands upon the wheel and soon the petite craft began to "walk the waters like a thing of life." Ball's excellent band was also there with wind and stringed instruments and soon the upper deck was cleared for "the mazes of the giddy dance" which passed off right merrily. The sky soon ceased weeping, the sun after a time glimmered through the clouds and Keuka, the fairest of little lakes in Western New York, smiled reciprocally under the sunlight. On sped the steamer—on went the dance—gay was the hilarity; and care seemed flung to the fresh morning breeze while cheerfulness and beaming mirth swayed the joyous crowd. At about 3 o'clock Hammondsport was reached and the company debarked and marched in procession to the hotel kept by Mr. A. Brundage where a bountiful and excellent repast was served up speedily for the benefit of nearly two hundred appreciative and remarkably hungry individuals. After which a dance was next in order in Mr. Brundage's ballroom which had been decorated and duly set in order. "The shades of night were falling fast" before the return trip was even thought of, when the company adjourned the dancing once more to the deck of the* Steuben *which was soon "homeward bound." The scenery along the shores of the lake was even more beautiful than by daylight— more grand and impressive at least. The sky was clear and lighted only by glimmering stars. On either hand rose wooded hills whose summits stood out in well defined but shadowy outlines against the horizon. The waves splashed and murmured faint music as the little steamer's bow cleft the water, and mingled weirdly with the gay sounds of the music and the innocent revelry on the upper deck. The engine puffed and clanked as if weary with its labor and from the smokestack flew up myriads of fiery sparks, eclipsing in brilliancy the stars and the uprising moon. To us, as we leaned idly over the rail, indulging in a contemplation of these blended scenes, the homeward trip was worth all the rest save—and we'll confess it frankly—the admirable dinner fixed up by Warner Cook, which infused new life and strength into the wearied frames of so many hungry folks!*

YATES COUNTY CHRONICLE, MAY 29, 1873

LAKE KEUKA—Our beautiful Keuka will yet inspire the song of the poet as few Lakes have, either in this country or in Europe. It is only just beginning to be appreciated by those residing near its picturesque shores. Tourists who have viewed the grand scenery of Switzerland, Italy, France, and other European countries, are most lavish in their praise of our own Lake Keuka scenery. The visitors from the cities of different States to this lake as a summer resort are largely increasing every year, and the indications are that its attractiveness will be enjoyed the coming summer by a far greater number of pleasure seekers than ever before. We hope to see multitudes come from all parts of the country, for the hotel accommodations in this village and at Grove Spring will surpass all previous seasons, and the Lake Keuka Steam Navigation Company are much better prepared to make it pleasant for all who ride on their fine steamers than they were last year, the high water enabling them to run their boats to the dock at the foot of Pine Street. The Steuben *has been dressed in handsome colors by artistic painters and starts out for business in elegant trim. The new steamer* Yates *which was built last year is to be repainted and tastefully furnished. She will be ready for service as soon as the season for travel is fully open. Visitors to the Watkins Glen cannot afford to miss a ride over Keuka on one of the company's handsome steamers, and a view of the majestic hills and fruitful vineyards about Hammondsport and we certainly think none of them will fail to visit our Lake.*

OVID INDEPENDENT, SEPTEMBER 23, 1873

The beautiful Lake Keuka, its banks almost covered with vineyards, groves, and cottages, just now affords a most delightful trip for travelers and excursionists. The grapes are rapidly ripening, several of the early varieties such as Delawares and Concords being now fully ripe. In about two weeks Catawbas, Dianas, and Isabellas will in many vineyards be fit to pick. The fine steamer Yates, *commanded by Capt. Thayer, and the* Steuben *commanded by Capt. Morse, each make daily the round trip of the lake and land passengers at any point desired. No more accommodating and courteous officers can be found anywhere. Those of our readers who would like to enjoy a fine autumn trip, should by all means try Lake Keuka. Take the Seneca Lake steamboats to Dresden, then the stage to Penn Yan and the lake. The thousands of acres of fruit-laden vineyards, the large wine cellars and the unsurpassed lake scenery cannot fail to interest and please all, especially strangers who have never hitherto visited them.*

YATES COUNTY CHRONICLE, JULY 2, 1874

KEUKA LAKE EXCURSION—The Academy excursion and pic-nic last Friday was a grand success. The day was an admirable one for a ride on Lake Keuka. Had it been furnished by a special providence it could hardly have been

Hammondsport Glen, in this postcard image, was part of the tour of Hammondsport.

finer. The company embarked in good season in the morning three hundred and fifty strong and arrived at Hammondsport at twelve o'clock. The time there was chiefly spent in partaking of dinner at the mouth of the Glen and the preparations requisite for comfort and convenience in that work. Notwithstanding some little disappointment in regard to the place for dining, as the size of the crowd had not been properly anticipated, the dinner passed off very pleasantly. All were bounteously provided for and all came away in the best of spirits. Nobody scolded except a few who were impatient that some were a little behind time at the boat, having lingered to take a look at the Glen.

We only wish there had been time for a general stroll of the whole party through the Glen. What was seen was much admired by those who went into it. Evidently the Glen is soon to become a very popular resort. Mr. J.P. Barnes has done a large amount of work to make it accessible and deserves encouragement for his enterprise. We hope to have it thronged with visitors before the close of the present season.

The return trip was quite as delightful as the upward voyage and all came home invigorated by one of the finest excursions that ever steamed over the Lake. A few moments were passed at Grove Spring on the down trip and all were much delighted with that charming public resort.

Nothing was omitted by the steamboat proprietors and steamboat officers to make the trip one of comfort and pleasure. The teachers of the Academy and schools were members of the party and most of the Board of Education. All voted the Academy pic-nic was an experience worth repeating when the proper occasion shall arrive.

YATES COUNTY CHRONICLE, JULY 6, 1876

On Lake Keuka, A Pleasant Pleasuring Party from Penn Yan—
*Music, Moonlight, Love and Flowers—Enjoyment Generally—Fortune
sometimes casts our lines in pleasant waters and nature yields bountifully to
our creel of pleasure, but it is very seldom that the good dame is so lavish of
her choice gifts as she was on the occasion of the grand musical excursion
and basket picnic from Penn Yan to Grove Spring and Hammondsport on
Wednesday, June 28th, into which we found ourselves unexpectedly, but
most delightfully, sandwiched.*

*We had been spending a few days in the pleasant village of Penn Yan,
enjoying the generous hospitality of some of its citizens. Bidding our friends
goodbye on Wednesday morning, we wended our way to the steamboat
landing when to our surprise, we found a multitude of pleasant people
onboard the steamer* Yates *and lining the shore along the dock.*

*The gentlemen and fair ladies of Penn Yan had turned out en masse
for a festal day on the limpid waters of lovely Lake Keuka. The excursion
was got up under the auspices of the Penn Yan Harmonic Union. The
party was composed of Hyatt's Military Band, the Penn Yan Quartet
Club, Miss Helen V. Bridgman, pianist, H.S. Bridgman, violinist,
Frank Phillips, cornet, E.H. Hopkins, alto, George S. Norris, basso,
Gillette's Orchestra, and about 300 more of Penn Yan's noblest citizens
and loveliest ladies.*

*The signal for starting was given, and amid charming music from the
band, the waving of handkerchiefs, and farewell adieus, the little boat
glided gracefully through the silver-crested waves of the lake on her way
to Grove Spring. The entire party was in the best of spirits and the ride
was a charming one. Close about us were whisperings of pleasure at the
scenes through which we passed, while all around us was a grand moving
panorama of picturesque hills, promontories, farm houses, woods and
vineyards that surpass in beauty and loveliness anything to be seen this side
of the Rocky Mountains. If any doubt this let them place themselves in as
pleasant a position as we were before deciding.*

*But we must not omit to mention that before leaving Penn Yan, the entire
command was assumed by that whole-souled commander, Farley Holmes,
whom everybody knows, which greatly enhanced the pleasure of everybody.*

*But too soon we arrived at Grove Spring where the party was cordially
received by the generous host and kind hostess of the Grove Spring House,
Mr. and Mrs. Laidlaw. Very soon the delicacies so bountifully provided*

for the occasion were spread on rustic tables scattered promiscuously about the shaded grounds that environ the Grove Spring House and render it so charming a resort, and over which all lingered with a sense of feeling for the time being at least, that verified the apocrypha "A man remembering neither sorrow nor debt" until it was announced that an outdoor concert would be given from the broad balcony of the Grove Spring House consisting of choruses, quartettes, &c., whither all hastened, when the highest acme of anticipated musical enjoyment was attained in listening to the music which arose with its voluptuous swell. We regret that we are not a musical critic, so as to do justice to the accomplished artists who so delightfully entertained their audience; but suffice it to say that the music was duly appreciated as was attested by the outburst of applause at the close of each piece. But we will take the liberty of saying that

Mrs. Tims, who sang a soprano solo in the last chorus, is possessed of rare musical talent, and the sweetness and melody of her voice were very pleasing. We might be tempted to give names of others did we know them; but on inquiry we learned that it was Miss Helen V. Bridgman who played the organ so finely.

But the time for departure from Grove Spring came at last and, embarking again on the little steamer for Hammondsport, the merry party was soon

This 1899 poster by the Erie Railroad was designed for the Rochester market. It shows departure times for all stops between Rochester and Bath.

124

gliding on the bosom of Lake Keuka, in admiration of the vine-clad hills that so beautifully surround the little lake. Arriving at Hammondsport, the party was welcomed by some of her pleasant citizens. Among them we noticed the Messers. Fairchild and their ladies, Messers. Rose, Davis, Switzer and others who escorted the party to Orchestrion Hall, when again the brightest hopes of festive pleasure were realized in the music, dancing and mild flirtation. After two more hours of unalloyed pleasure, the party started on their homeward journey.

In behalf of the entire company, thanks are tendered to Commodore Farley Holmes, Captain Thayer, and Mr. and Mrs. Laidlaw for their exceeding kindness.

YATES COUNTY CHRONICLE, JULY 18, 1878

MOONLIGHT TRIP TO GROVE SPRING—The excursion last Tuesday night on the steamer Yates by the K.B. Club and their friends to Grove Spring was a very pleasant, quiet, social affair and may be pronounced an unmitigated success. The start was made in the cool of the evening and the sail up was rendered delightful by a refreshing breeze and by the sweet sounds evoked by Hyatt's Band which accompanied the excursionists. As the boat rounded Bluff Point, the scene was lighted up by the full-orbed, rising moon and the towering Bluff and the opposing hills covered with a light haze, with the two arms of the lake stretching back into obscurity, made a picture of enchantment that seemed to need but a touch of some fairy's wand to cause it to dissolve from mortal vision. Shortly after the arrival of the Yates at Grove Spring, the steamer Lulu brought another delegation of equal size and merit. The combined parties were soon merrily engaged in the dance to the music of Ball's full orchestra. At about twelve o'clock the company entered upon the equally pleasant task of disposing of a most substantial and tastefully gotten up repast prepared by mine host Cole of the Grove Spring House. After a short return to dancing, the parties repaired to their respective boats and the Penn Yan delegation was soon landed in the quiet village streets at a moderately early hour of the morning, little the worse for wear and well satisfied with the success of the trip.

YATES COUNTY CHRONICLE, JUNE 19, 1895

The Penn Yan Band will give the first big moonlight ride on the Mary
Bell *on the evening of July 2. The boat will stop at Keuka College,
Elmwood, Fenton's, Crosby's, Keuka, Gibson's and Branchport and 25¢
is the very low round trip fare for this first trip. The band still owes
about $100 on their new instruments and thus this benefit is gotten up.
Remember the boat will be gorgeously decorated with colored lights and
will return at 12 o'clock.*

Lemonade and ice cream were served on board to over three hundred
people. The band netted seventy-five dollars.

Also in that summer of 1895 was the ultimate moonlight cruise. Harry Morse,
captain of the *Mary Bell,* had the idea for what was billed as the Monster
Moonlight Excursion. One steamboat, the *Holmes,* left Hammondsport at
the end of the southern branch of the lake loaded with people. At the same
time, the *Halsey* left from Branchport at the end of the west branch also at
full capacity. A third, the *Mary Bell,* left the steamboat dock in Penn Yan.
The three boats met off the end of Bluff Point. The other two were lashed
to the sides of the *Mary Bell,* platforms were put between them and strings
of lights were put up to add to the occasion. The people, who paid all of
twenty-five cents for a ticket, moved freely between the three boats and the
three bands. The *Mary Bell* slowly powered them from the end of the bluff
to Hammondsport and then returned while they dined and danced. The
1,800 people on board the three boats didn't get home until well after 3:00
a.m. the next morning.

Not all outings on the boats were pleasant. There were occasional
fights on board, usually fueled by alcohol. At such times, the captain of
the boat might stop at some landing along the lake and let the disorderly
person(s) off for a long walk through the woods back to town. Other
times, the crew would hold the person until the boat got back to Penn
Yan or Hammondsport, and the sheriff would be contacted. One
incident of note occurred in September 1911. At that time, all the towns
in Yates County voted "no license," which meant no alcoholic beverages
could be sold. The Town of Wayne in Steuben County, however, voted
"license," so alcohol was readily available in the hotels at Keuka village.
There was a regular flow of people taking the steamers from Penn Yan
to the Keuka Hotel. The *Yates County Chronicle* reported in an article in

The *Halsey* docked at Keuka College.

September 1911, "Another outrageous drunken revel occurred at Keuka Sunday. This has become of such common occurrence at that place that people in that neighborhood say that it is a regular 'hell' on Sundays." Two intoxicated men got on the *Steuben* to come back to Penn Yan and insulted a few of the women on board. Their male companions took issue with that, and a mêlée ensued. One man was knocked unconscious, and when Captain Howard Stone tried to stop the altercation, he was knocked down. The boat hands swung into action, and the "drunken loafers" were overpowered and tied up with ropes. The *Steuben* stopped at Keuka College, and the sheriff was called. Both men were eventually sentenced to thirty days in the Yates County jail.

The week following the incident, a letter appeared in the *Chronicle*:

> *The disgraceful conditions which have existed at Keuka since the town of Wayne voted license have been a burning disgrace to the citizens of that township. The drunkenness, fighting and rowdyism at Keuka on Sundays as well as other days have kept many good citizens from stopping there and it must be a source of worriment to the decent, law-abiding residents of that locality who are compelled to submit to such disgraceful conditions. Aside from the annoyance caused them, Penn Yan and other places have also been*

annoyed by the drunks returning from Keuka, and it is to be hoped there is sufficient loyalty and pride among the voters of the town of Wayne to get out on election day and vote out this curse, which is a blot on the beautiful township of Wayne.—A Milo Citizen

Chapter 7

GRAPES AND WINE

From mid-September until late November, the steamboat companies shifted their emphasis from the summer excursionists to freight. Most of the freight consisted of farm products, and the most profitable of these were grapes.

The growth of vineyards around the lake coincided with the growth of the steamboat business, and the grapes and the steamers mutually benefited each other. An Episcopal minister in Hammondsport, Reverend William Bostwick, is usually given credit for planting the first grapevines in his yard in the 1820s. After the vines were established, he gave cuttings to his neighbors, and grape farming then spread northward along the shores of the lake through Urbana to Wayne, Pulteney and eventually Yates County. In 1870, there were 3,000 acres of vines in the Hammondsport area; twenty years later, there were 14,500.[36]

Farmers at first only marketed the grapes on a local basis, and early attempts to ship them out of the area to New York City, for example, were ineffective; travel connections were too slow, and there were few agents to handle the sale and distribution. That changed dramatically in the decades following the Civil War. With the completion of the Bath & Hammondsport Railroad to the head of the lake on the southern end in 1875 and the Fall Brook/New York Central to the foot of the lake in Penn Yan in 1884, an effective transportation network existed. It wasn't long before businessmen such as Samuel McMath and William Wise in Penn Yan or Trevor Moore and the Lyon brothers in Hammondsport saw the potential profits in handling the shipping and marketing of the area's grapes. Warehouses for storage and packinghouses were built. Factories for making grape boxes and baskets became a major industry around the lake. In 1870, 350,000 boxes were needed for shipping grapes.[37] In 1909, William Wise claimed that he shipped one thousand boxcars of grapes out of Penn Yan. Grapes and the businesses that supported them became a major factor in the area's economy.

The grapes grown in the nineteenth century were considered "native varieties" such as Isabellas, Concords, Catawbas, Ionas, Dianas, Niagaras and Delawares. The vast majority of them were harvested and shipped as table grapes, but where there are grapes, there will soon be wine. Once again, Reverend Bostwick in Hammondsport led the way by making sacramental wine for his church and talking to his farmer neighbors about winemaking. The first wine was shipped out of the area in 1857 by Josiah Prentiss of Pulteney under the name Highland Cottage Wine.

The first large-scale operations for winemaking developed in the Pleasant Valley south of Hammondsport on the eve of the Civil War by the Hammondsport Wine Company and the Pleasant Valley Wine Company. Other wineries like Germania later were started there. The first winery along the lakeshore, however, was the Urbana Wine Company, founded in 1865. It held New York State's bonded winery license #2; license #1 was held by the Pleasant Valley Winery. The winery was built along the western shore of the lake about three miles out of the village of Hammondsport, located there for direct access to the lake steamers. The community that formed around it, mainly housing the workers and their families, became known as Urbana. The winery brought in winemakers from the Champagne region of France and focused on champagne and other sparkling wine. It developed the Gold Seal brand in the 1880s, and Gold Seal Champagne became its best-selling product. It also produced clarets, ports and catawbas. The Urbana Wine Company was the premier winery on the lake during the steamboat era. In the 1950s, it became the Gold Seal Winery and continued to produce fine wine into the 1980s. In 1983, it was bought by Seagram's, which shut down the winery. Once considered the most picturesque winery on the lake, the building is seriously deteriorated as of this writing.

A few miles south of Urbana along the western shore of the lake was the Lake Keuka Wine Company. The winery was next to Gibson's Landing, opposite the end of Bluff Point. George Gibson was one of the founders of the company and oversaw construction of the building, using stone brought by steamboat from Keuka Park. It produced a variety of wine and received this critique in 1884:

The Urbana Wine Company building shown here still exists but no longer as an active winery. It was known for the Gold Seal brand.

The Port wines of this company are noted especially for their purity. The difference between this port and any imitation or compound wine is that the latter always deposits a sediment, while the Keuka draws clear and bright until the bottom is in sight. The Keuka Sherry is pure, cheap, and better in quality than most of the sherry throughout the country. Their sweet and dry Catawbas and Isabellas are superb. Their Claret is a favorite and satisfying beverage and their Brandy can be conscientiously commended for medicinal and social use as pure in every respect.[38]

In the summer of 1884, the Lake Keuka Wine Company introduced a champagne that was fermented in the bottles, which is the French style. It became a major seller. In 1902, the company reorganized under new ownership with the name White Top Winery, focusing solely on the production of champagne. White Top advertised that it was the only exclusively champagne producer in America. Another claim to fame it had was that it was the only Finger Lakes winery successfully raided by federal officers during Prohibition. Actually, it was raided twice by federal agents. The second time, in November 1925, over eighteen thousand gallons of champagne, wine and brandy were poured into the lake. The main building of the White Top Winery burned to the ground in a spectacular fire in the summer of 1955. It was in operation until that time.

The largest winery on the Penn Yan end of the lake was the Empire State Wine Company, organized by two Penn Yan businessmen. The wine company was organized in 1896, and that same year, the founders built a beautiful three-story building near where the steamers entered the outlet. The Empire State Winery became a major landmark on that end of the lake. It produced State Seal Champagne, along with brandy and other still wines. It was the first winery in the area to have tours so the public could see how wine is produced. The company survived Prohibition in the 1920s by producing grape juice and wine for both medicinal and religious uses. It kept many local men employed through the Depression of the 1930s but finally closed its doors in 1944. The historic building was bought by the American Legion in the early 1950s and used by it for nearly forty years. In the late 1980s, the building and land were sold to a developer who planned to raze the old building. Despite a major campaign to preserve the landmark, it was torn down in 1990.

Wine was shipped on the steamboats when it was ready, but the grape harvest was in the autumn of the year. Vineyardists picked their grapes, put them in boxes and took them to packinghouses, where they would be put into baskets. The baskets were then taken to the nearest dock to

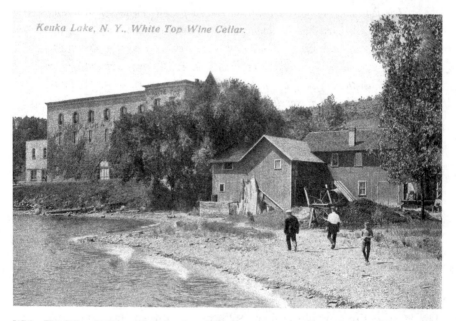

Keuka Lake, N. Y., White Top Wine Cellar.

White Top Wine Cellar produced only sparkling wines. The main building still stands beside Route 54A on Keuka's west side.

The Empire State Winery property in Penn Yan, at the mouth of the outlet, included acres of grapes and orchards. The cupola on top of the winery could be seen for miles down the lake and was used as a navigation aid by the steamboats.

await the steamboat. John McMath, who followed his father, Samuel, in the grape shipping business, recalled that at the peak of the harvest, it was necessary for four steamers to make two trips to each side of the lake to bring the grapes to the shipping point in Penn Yan. Starting early in the morning, the last boat would often come to the warehouse after 9:00 p.m. It was mainly due to Samuel McMath's efforts that a lighthouse was put up at the entrance to the outlet. The baskets of grapes were removed from the steamers and loaded onto ventilated boxcars of the Fall Brook Railroad. On one day in October 1915, the steamer *Penn Yan* carried 22,000 baskets of grapes into Penn Yan. Each rail car held a minimum of 1,250 baskets. McMath estimated that 60 percent of the income of Yates County came from the grape trade during the peak years, as 100,000 baskets a day passed through Penn Yan.[39] In October 1895, the steamer *Urbana* carried 1,602 picking boxes of grapes to the Smith & Lyon warehouse in Hammondsport, which was a record amount for one boat at that time.[40] The grapes leaving Penn Yan traveled on the "Fruit Trains," and the ones leaving Hammondsport traveled the "Champagne Route." Keuka Lake grapes and wine were marketed all over the country.

The following article from the *Yates County Chronicle* of October 1, 1874, further tells the story:

Most farmers packed their grapes in pony baskets for rail shipment to city markets. These handcarts, provided by the steamship lines, facilitated transfer of the grape baskets from dock to steamboat to rail car.

Vintage Time on the Shores of Keuka—Reader, have you ever visited Lake Keuka and its places of interest—Grove Spring, Urbana, Hammondsport, Pleasant Valley &c— in vintage time? Well, if you have or haven't, don't fail to do so this fall; and as the season is nearly two weeks ahead of the ordinaries, the trip should not be postponed later than from the 10th to the 12th of October, if you should behold the vintage in all its unrivaled richness and glory.

There is nothing like it on this continent and but few, if any, similar scenes that surpass it in the Old World. From the vicinity of Bluff Point, some seven miles north of Hammondsport, to the Pleasant Valley wine cellars, two miles south of the head of the lake in the direction of Bath, the amount of grapes produced this year is well nigh incredible. Bluff Point on its eastern, southern, and western slopes, both shores of the lake from there to Hammondsport and north of Urbana, stretching away for miles toward Branchport, is an almost continuous vineyard which, with those in Pleasant Valley, if laid out half a mile wide would probably extend a distance of not less than twenty miles. Only think of it!

Ten square miles of grapes in full bearing and embracing every approved variety beneath the sun! The hillsides at this gladsome season of the year are alive with men, women, and children picking grapes. The steamboat docks are

This advertisement in 1900 for Hammondsport excursions does not include a steamboat ride, as did previous posters.

piled with grapes in crates, the steamers are loaded down with them, the roadways leading to the landings and wine cellars are thronged with teams drawing grapes by the ton for wine making and marketing.

The picture presented at Urbana (four miles north of Hammondsport on the west shore of the lake) and at Pleasant Valley, where all the processes of wine making may be seen by visitors can neither be imagined nor adequately described. We would not be surprised to learn two months hence that Urbana has crushed over 1,000 tons of grapes this year, Pleasant Valley not less than 1,500 and that other hundreds of tons have been disposed of by smaller establishments of which there are quite a number in the grape growing region. According to present appearances, the finest stock ever laid in by the two great wine companies above mentioned, in any one year, will flow from the vintage of 1874 and the fame of their leading and popular brands be fully maintained in all coming years. These are the Great Western and Carte Blanche of Pleasant Valley (awarded the highest gold medal premium at Vienna in 1873) and the Gold Seal and Imperial of Urbana (awarded the grand diploma of honor at the same exhibition on the Industry of All Nations).

The best place to locate for a week's study of the Keuka grape region in vintage time is at the Grove Spring House, Col. Stephen Moore, proprietor, assisted by his son Forrie G. in the office and Admiral Thad, the champion oarsman of the lake. This house is delightfully located on the east side of

135

A 1912 postcard view of the Gibson House at Gibson's Landing.

the lake nearly opposite the Urbana cellars. That attractive stop, as well as Bluff Point, Hammondsport and its beautiful and romantic glen, Pleasant Valley and all other places of interest, including the best hunting and fishing grounds, can be reached only by steamers and by sail and rowboats. I but speak from the record in saying that there is not in all the state a more charming place for an October sojourn for a few days or longer than at the Grove Spring House which is kept open until the middle of November. And no more hospitable, generous and genial gentleman on this side of the planet than Superintendent Switzer and W.A. Tomer of Urbana and Superintendent Champlin and Messers Bauder and French of Pleasant Valley.—M.Ells, Esq.

Chapter 8

THE END OF AN ERA

The year 1915 could rightly be designated as the end of the steamboat era on Keuka Lake. Of the last three steamers, the *Penn Yan* was fitted with gasoline engines in 1915, and the *Steuben* and *Yates* were condemned at the end of the season. Grove Springs, the largest resort on the lake, burned to the ground that December. Long gone were the Ark, O-go-ya-go and the Idlewild Hotel. Local newspapers were commenting that there were more automobiles in downtown Penn Yan than there were horses. State highways were being built to connect Penn Yan with Dundee, Branchport and Dresden. The automobile age was well underway. A fitting eulogy for the end of the era appeared in the *Yates County Chronicle* of March 3, 1915, under the headline "NEW FLEET OF STEAMERS TO SAIL ON LAKE KEUKA":

> *And they died alone among friends. Their last whistles echoed through the grape-lined hills to an uncomprehending people. Everyone thought that the long escape of musical steam at the Hammondsport waterfront marked but another hibernation. They knew not that the steamers* Steuben *and* Yates, *and the freighter* Springstead, *were entering their final sleep. For comes word from the Erie railroad officials that never more will these boats breathe with steaming life again. A rejuvenated steamer* Penn Yan *and two new steel passenger and freight barges of the most modern types will care for this summer's business.*
>
> *For thirty-two springs and summers and falls had the* Yates *parted the waters of Lake Keuka to gather its grapes for hungry railroad outlets or the clamoring presses of the great champagne cellars and to carry the sons*

of the Southern Tier counties for business and pleasure upon its bosom. The larger Steuben was four years younger, but its big sidewheels had churned the waters from Hammondsport to Pulteney to Penn Yan, first as a commercial enemy, next as an able partner, then as a senior partner.

The Holmes and the Halsey they were in the beginning and the Holmes and the Halsey they are to this day to hundreds of revering people. They were born in a day when the shores and hotels of this most beautiful lake in western New York overflowed with resident anglers and pleasure-seekers. They died in a day when passenger traffic has declined in the face of automobiles. No, the charge is untrue. They had not outlived their usefulness. They were as safe to travelers as ever. They are simply the victims of twentieth century demand. Each year had exacted a toll from them. They had slowed up while the world was insisting on greater speed. The time had arrived when they were too expensive, too out of date, too crude.

The history of yesterday repeated itself; the old must give way to the new. So had passed the early canalers and the first Steuben and Yates. So had gone the graceful-lined Urbana and the never-to-be-forgotten Lulu, which gave the longest ride per mile of any boat that was ever on the lake. So had the throaty West Branch and the lively Cricket journeyed into the beyond. It is not so much that these old steamers are condemned as worthless hulks by the inviolable law of time, though that will be sad news to the thousands who have ridden upon and loved them, but rather that they should have become grim, dead emblems of the past without the obsequies that were their due.

What is to be done with them is now unknown to the Erie officials themselves. They are absolutely valueless to the railroad outside of their engines and furnishings. Perhaps they will be eventually cremated. Their corpses would make a wonderful bonfire and illuminate Bluff Point and other of Keuka's hills with an effect that would perpetuate their memory.

It will be a different steamer Penn Yan that will start at the opening of navigation the forepart of April. About $12,000 is transforming this beautiful lake boat so it will hardly be recognized. The upper deck in front of the pilot house is to be removed and the pilot house, or "director's room" as some have laughingly referred to it owing to its unusual size, will be placed on a level with the second deck, or rather a new and smaller one will be. This will give the pilot a fine view ahead. Two new 100-horsepower gasoline engines will be the motive force and will give the boat increased speed. The purser's quarters will be further in the rear than now, with the engines directly in front of it. This will leave a large, open bow, roomy, airy

*and nice for passengers and ample for freight. The boat will draw ten inches
less water, making the channel at Penn Yan less dangerous to it.*

Complaints against the Erie Railroad started soon after the 1911 sinking
of the *Steuben* at the dock at Hammondsport because of the lack of proper
maintenance. At the end of the 1912 grape harvest, the *Hammondsport
Herald* reported:

> *Boat Service Criticized—For some reason the Lake Keuka steamers have
> been unable to handle the grapes as expeditiously this fall as usual. In many
> cases it has been necessary to deliver grapes to dealers here by teams from as
> far down the lake as Keuka. Complaint is made that grapes have laid on
> the docks for days before being transported. It is said that the main difficulty
> has been to get sufficient and efficient help, and this in turn is accounted for
> in the fact that the wages paid by the company are so low that efficient help
> cannot be secured during the busy vintage season.*

The next year, the Erie Company sent life preservers for the steamer
Steuben that had been on its ferryboats in New York Harbor. They failed state
inspection. The *Hammondsport Herald* reported:

> *If the Erie Company only had the sense to run the B&H trains and
> Lake Keuka Navigation Company boats on business principles, with
> a resident manager with some authority to meet local conditions, the
> companies would make a lot more money and the patrons would be fairly
> well satisfied. Such a railroad as the B&H and such a traffic as that on
> Lake Keuka cannot reasonably be operated on the rules and management
> of trunk lines and big water routes. The business here is principally
> local and unless local conditions are fairly met, the business must be
> unsatisfactory and unprofitable.*

Since the Erie Railroad also owned the railroad between Bath and
Hammondsport, the dissatisfaction was particularly strong on the Penn Yan
end of the lake. The *Yates County Chronicle* complained about the boat schedule
as it related to Penn Yan in July 1913: "The trouble with the schedule is that
it does not give prospective customers or lake visitors time enough between
boats to do any shopping at the Penn Yan end of the lake while there seems
to be plenty of time given at Hammondsport. Neither do the boats connect
with the New York Central or Northern Central trains at Penn Yan."

The new, "improved" *Penn Yan* did not have a long life. It was noisy and smelly and vibrated with gasoline engines instead of the steam engine for which it was designed.

The conversion made to the *Penn Yan* (formerly the *Mary Bell*) did not work out well. Local people did not like the changes made to the former Queen of Keuka, especially the new gasoline engines. "The changes made in the *Penn Yan* will not increase the popularity of that boat as a passenger steamer. We are told there is a constant trembling of the boat while it is in motion. One person said a few days ago that it would shake false teeth out of your mouth if you had any."[41]

Neither did the two gasoline-powered steel boats the Erie built capture the imagination of the public. The *City of Rochester* was launched in May 1915, and the *Yates County Chronicle* reported in July, "The *City of Rochester*, the new steamer on Lake Keuka, started running last week and it looks rather odd compared to the boats that have been seen on the lake so many years. From its architecture it is assumed it will not be in the speedy class, nor will it take a prize at a beauty show." It *was* slow, taking over four hours to go from Hammondsport to Penn Yan (the old *Urbana* made the trip once in less than an hour and a half), and it *was* ugly. People along the lakeshore called the *City of Rochester* "the Potato Bug" because it looked like one. It was obvious to people that the Erie was deemphasizing passenger traffic and was going to concentrate on freight. The second boat, the *City of Elmira*, was launched in October and received similar reviews. One letter to the editor of the *Chronicle* wrote that neither boat honored the cities they were meant to honor.

The *City of Rochester* and the *City of Elmira* (seen here at Keuka Hotel dock) replaced the steamboats to bring grapes to market. They were not suited for passengers and never achieved the popularity of the steamboats.

In April 1917, President Woodrow Wilson asked Congress for a declaration of war against Germany, and the United States joined the Great War in Europe. Business and profits increased dramatically for the nation's railroads as they became vital to the war effort. The Erie Railroad cut back even further boat service on Lake Keuka. The *Corning Leader* complained in August that there was no rail connection between Bath and the lake; the only way to get there was by bus. The only boats operating on the lake in 1917 were the *Rochester* and the *Elmira*. Only one boat a day went between Hammondsport and Penn Yan every day except Sundays.

In 1918, the Erie Railroad announced that there would be no boat service on the lake at all and probably never again. There was a general outcry in the area, but the people hardest hit were the vineyardists around the lake.

> *Many of them have no wagons or even horses fit to draw their product to market and even so, the roads for which they have heretofore had no use are almost impassable on account of the extremely steep hills and for lack of attention or repairs. This class of vineyardists has for many years depended entirely upon the boats operated on the lake for their transportation to Penn Yan and Hammondsport, and especially for reaching market with their grapes.*[42]

William Wise is shown here in front of his office inspecting a load of grapes.

Already hurt by wartime labor shortages, with national Prohibition becoming closer to reality and with no rail connection in Hammondsport, the vineyardists put pressure on Penn Yan's biggest grape shipper, William Wise. Wise, who also happened to be the Yates County fuel administrator (wartime measure), had a little influence in Washington. In the summer, representatives of the Railroad Administration, Division of Inland Waterways (another wartime measure), came to Lake Keuka to look over the situation and report back to Washington. In late summer, it was announced that two remaining boats, the *Rochester* and the *Elmira*, would be taken over and operated by the federal government starting in late September. They continued to operate the boats until the end of the year to allow for people to get to Penn Yan for Christmas shopping. In the summer of 1919, there was no boat service whatsoever, leading the *Yates County Chronicle* to complain that August:

> *The influx of visitors to Lake Keuka this season's been greater than in many years, despite the lack of facilities for getting back and forth from cottages which are not located along the trolley or near a good automobile road. The only way to win people to all parts of the lake is to have a service which will enable them to get there. All about Bluff Point for several miles in any direction are the beauty spots of the lake. Never is the scene tiresome, but it has been so inaccessible as to lose popularity.*

A small, privately owned boat, the *Onalinda*, with a capacity of forty passengers, stepped in toward the end of the 1919 season to fill the void, but that was just for a few months. Later that autumn, the Erie Railroad sold the last of its boats, the *City of Rochester* and the *City of Elmira*, to the Garrett Wine Company, which used them mainly for freight in the 1920s. Except for a very brief comeback for the *Penn Yan* in 1922, the era of the big boats on Lake Keuka was over.

NOTES

CHAPTER 2

1. *Yates County Chronicle*, February 22, 1872.
2. Ibid., March 7, 1872.

CHAPTER 3

3. Hamlin, "Reminiscences of Lake Keuka."
4. *Chronicle-Express*, July 6, 1944.
5. *Illustrated Buffalo Express*, Summer 1891.

CHAPTER 4

6. *Yates County Chronicle*, September 7, 1865.
7. Harvey, *Building America's Main Street*.
8. *Penn Yan Express*, June 13, 1883.
9. *Yates County Chronicle*, December 26, 1917. Letter by Theodore O. Hamlin.

10. Don Quant, article in the *Copper Nail* (newsletter of the Finger Lakes Boating Museum), March 2009.

11. *Yates County Chronicle*, November 14, 1917. Letter by T.O. Hamlin.

12. Alderman Gleason (Wayne town historian), *Steuben Farmer's Advocate* (Bath, NY), n.d.

13. *Yates County Chronicle*, August 22, 1906.

14. *Hammondsport Herald*, March 22, 1911.

15. *Yates County Chronicle*, June 15, 1904.

16. Ibid., October 10, 1907.

17. *Penn Yan Express*, September 5, 1894.

18. *Yates County Chronicle*, June 17, 1908.

CHAPTER 5

19. *Hammondsport Herald*, May 5, 1885.

20. *American Magazine*, "Lacustrine Leaves."

21. *Yates County Chronicle*, May 13, 1913.

22. Ibid., April 3, 1878.

23. *Chronicle-Express*, "Recalls Days When Keuka Lake Boat Became Famous Ark" (memories of John M. Jensen), February 24, 1938.

24. *Hammondsport Herald*.

25. Ibid., February 9, 1912.

26. Ibid.

27. Ibid., August 8, 1883.

28. Morris, *Mountain and Lake Resorts*.

29. Nykiel, *Brief History of the Keuka Hotel*.

30. *Keuka Hotel on Lake Keuka*, promotional booklet, 1913.

31. *Elmira (NY) Sunday Telegram*, 1966.

32. *Sunday Spectator (Hornell, NY)*, 1974.

33. *Chronicle-Express*, July 16, 1942.

34. *Yates County Chronicle*, December 15, 1915.

35. *Crooked Lake Review*, "Beautiful Keuka Lake: Elmira Daily Advertiser, Saturday, 26 July 1902," Summer 2005.

CHAPTER 7

36. Sherer, "Finger Lakes Grape Pioneers."
37. Sherer, *Crooked Lake and the Grape*.
38. *Keuka: Lakeside Life in Central New York*. Leve and Alden's Publication Department, 1884.
39. Bellis, *Recollections of John E. McMath*.
40. *Hammondsport Herald*, October 23, 1895.

CHAPTER 8

41. *Penn Yan Democrat,* July 16, 1915.
42. Ibid., August 1918.

BIBLIOGRAPHY

American Magazine (Frank Leslie's Popular Monthly). "Lacustrine Leaves" by "An Old Cornellian." 1888.

Bellis, Vincent J., Jr., ed. *Recollections of John E. McMath.* "Sam, That Was My Last Car." Yates County History Center.

Elmira Advertiser. "Hammondsport: Its Orchestrion and Orchestrian Hall." May 1876. *Crooked Lake Review,* August 1992. www.crookedlakereview.com.

Elmira Daily Advertiser. "Beautiful Keuka Lake." July 26, 1902. Reprinted in *Crooked Lake Review,* Summer 2005. www.crookedlakereview.com.

Gordon, William Reed. *Keuka Lake Memories.* Interlaken, NY: Heart of the Lakes Publishing, 1986.

"Grove Spring House from the Hammondsport Herald." *Crooked Lake Review,* July 1989. www.crookedlakereview.com.

Hakes, Harlo. *Landmarks of Steuben County.* N.p.: D. Mason and Company, 1896.

Hamlin, Theodore O. "Reminiscences of Lake Keuka." April 1934. Collection of the Yates County History Center.

Hammond, Samuel H. "Bluff Point and Keuka Lake, 1855." *Crooked Lake Review*, September 1990. www.crookedlakereview.com.

———. "Penn Yan and Keuka Lake, 1855." *Crooked Lake Review*, August 1990. www.crookedlakereview.com.

Hammondsport Herald. "The *Mary Bell*: The Queen of Lake Keuka." May 1892. Reprinted in *Crooked Lake Review*, July 1989. www.crookedlakereview.com.

Harvey, Steven. *Building America's Main Street, Not Wall Street.* Bloomington, IN: AuthorHouse, 2010.

———. *It Started with a Steamboat: An American Saga.* Bloomington, IN: AuthorHouse, 2007.

Keuka: Lakeside Life in Central New York. New York: Leve & Alden's Publications Department, 1884.

Mitchell, Charles R. *Hammondsport and Keuka Lake.* Dover, NH: Arcadia Publishing, 1998.

———. *Keuka Lake.* Charleston, SC: Arcadia Publishing, 2002.

———. *Penn Yan and Keuka Lake.* Dover, NH: Arcadia Publishing, 1997.

Mitchell, Charles R., and Kirk W. House. *Corning.* Charleston, SC: Arcadia Publishing, 2003.

Morris, Nelson Hapgood. *Mountain and Lake Resorts: A Chance Courtship.* N.p.: Lackawanna Railroad, 1904.

Nykiel, Vincent L. *A Brief History of the Keuka Hotel and the Keuka Hotel Dance Hall.* N.p., 2001.

Palmer, Richard F. "The Bath & Hammondsport Railroad." *Crooked Lake Review*, November 1994. www.crookedlakereview.com.

Quant, Don. "News and Notes on *Cricket*, 1894 to 1909." Collection of the Yates County History Center.

Sherer, Richard G. *Crooked Lake and the Grape*. Virginia Beach, VA: Donning Company, 1998.

———. "Finger Lakes Grape Pioneers." *Crooked Lake Review*, January 1989. www.crookedlakereview.com.

———. *Steuben County: The First 200 Years*. Virginia Beach, VA: Donning Company, 1996.

Swartout, Laura L. *A History of Hammondsport to 1962*. N.p.: Corning-Painted Post Historical Society, 1962.

Toaspern, Annette. *Willow Grove*. N.p.: Expressly Yours Press, 2011.

Treicher, Bill. "The Grove Springs Hotel." *Crooked Lake Review*, July 1989. www.crookedlakereview.com.

Wolcott, Walter. *Penn Yan, New York*. N.p.: Peerless Printing Company, 1914.

INDEX

A

Arey, Albert 99
Ark, the 54, 67, 73, 79, 84, 85, 86, 87, 88, 89, 90, 91, 137
Around the Loop 76, 106

B

Ball, Dr. George H. 93
Bath & Hammondsport Railroad 24, 28, 32, 33, 43, 47, 49, 56, 72, 79, 109, 112, 115, 129
Bimini Springs 90
Bostwick, William W. 21, 129, 130
Branchport 12, 23, 28, 47, 54, 58, 75, 76, 77, 91, 94, 105, 106, 107, 113, 126, 134, 137

C

Care Naught 30, 34, 49, 109
Carpenter, Calvin 39, 88, 89, 90
Central Point 70, 99
City of Elmira 140, 143
City of Rochester 140, 143
Conklin, Frank 49, 53, 54, 58, 75

Cornell, John 76, 77
Corning Landing 115
Cricket (1894–1909) 58, 72, 73, 74, 75, 76, 77, 83, 106, 138
Crooked Lake Canal 17, 22, 28, 37, 43, 81
Crooked Lake Navigation Company 31, 32, 33, 50, 54, 56, 65
Crooked Lake Steamboat Company 17, 37
Crosby 62, 95
Crosby, Joseph 25, 26, 27, 42, 43, 95

D

Dewey, David E. 89, 90
Drake, Charles W. 33, 34, 48, 49, 54, 56, 57, 58, 65, 67, 72, 75, 108, 109, 112
Drake, James 108
Drake's Point 107
Dresden 17, 23, 43, 86, 96, 121, 137

E

Eggleston Glen 98, 99
Electric Park 94

Elms 114
Empire State Wine Company 132
Erie Railroad 22, 23, 25, 34, 50, 54,
    58, 70, 71, 72, 75, 76, 116, 118,
    137, 139, 141, 143

F

Fairchild, Ed 115, 116
Fairchild House 115, 116
Fall Brook Railroad 23, 79, 81, 85,
    105, 133
Finton's Landing 53, 95

G

Gibson, George 108, 109, 130
Gibson's Landing 24, 54, 58, 61, 62,
    108, 126, 130
Gleason, Hiram 16, 34, 109
Gold Seal 21, 114, 130, 135
grapes 21, 59, 61, 77, 80, 95, 105, 107,
    115, 121, 129, 130, 132, 133,
    134, 135, 137, 139, 141
Green, Seth 100
Gregg, John 17, 18, 37, 39, 119
Grove Springs 27, 34, 44, 52, 99, 109,
    110, 111, 112, 114, 121, 122,
    123, 125, 134, 137
Grove Springs Hotel 30, 31, 52, 67, 72,
    75, 110, 112, 114, 124, 135, 136
G.R. Youngs/Steuben (II) (1865–79) 19,
    25, 26, 27, 40, 41, 42, 43, 47

H

Halsey, Helen 33, 56, 57, 65
Halsey/Steuben (III) (1887–1915) 32, 49,
    53, 56, 58, 59, 61, 62, 67, 83,
    126, 138
Halsey, William L. 30, 31, 32, 34, 49,
    50, 51, 52, 54, 56, 109
Hamlin, Theodore O. 30, 32, 33, 50,
    56, 57, 65
Hammondsport 17, 18, 21, 22, 23, 24,
    25, 26, 28, 31, 32, 37, 39, 41,
    42, 46, 47, 48, 49, 50, 52, 53,
    54, 56, 58, 59, 62, 63, 65, 67,
    70, 72, 75, 76, 77, 79, 81, 85,
    88, 99, 105, 107, 108, 109, 110,
    115, 117, 120, 121, 122, 123,
    124, 125, 126, 129, 130, 133,
    134, 135, 136, 137, 138, 139,
    140, 141, 142
Hammondsport Glen 116
Helvetia House 104
Hermit of the Lone Pine 60
Holmes, Farley 26, 28, 29, 30, 42, 43,
    51, 123, 125
Holmes/Yates (II) (1883–1915) 31, 32,
    49, 50, 51, 52, 53, 54, 56, 58,
    59, 62, 67, 85, 86, 107, 126, 138

I

Idlewild 47, 53, 95, 96, 97, 98, 137

J

Jolly 44

K

Keuka (1835–48) 17, 37, 39, 88
Keuka Club 110
Keuka College 24, 63, 68, 79, 85,
    126, 127
Keuka Hotel 75, 99, 100, 101, 103,
    104, 109, 112, 126
Keuka (II) (1867–74) 26, 27, 42, 43
Keuka Lake Transit Company 76
Keuka Landing 61, 100, 104, 105
Keuka Park 75, 91, 92, 94, 130
Keuka Steamboat Company 28, 29,
    46, 48
Knapp, Oliver C. 31, 32

L

Lake Keuka Navigation Company
    (LKNC) 26, 27, 29, 30, 32, 33,
    42, 49, 52, 56, 57, 65, 70, 72,
    75, 112, 115, 139
Lake Keuka Wine Company 108, 109,
    130, 131